5 STEPS TO

Christian Growth

LEADER'S GUIDE

Bill Bright

NewLife
PUBLICATIONS
A MINISTRY OF CAMPUS CRUSADE FOR CHRIST

Five Steps of Christian Growth:
Leader's Guide

Published by
New*Life* Publications
375 Highway 74 South, Suite A
Peachtree, GA 30269

Printed in the United States of America

ISBN: 1-56399-022-9

Distributed in Canada by Campus Crusade for Christ of Canada, Surrey, B.C.

Unless otherwise indicated, all Scripture references are taken from the *New International Version*, © 1973, 1978, 1984 by the International Bible Society. Published by Zondervan Bible Publishers, Grand Rapids, Michigan.

Scripture quotations designated TLB are from *The Living Bible,* © 1971 by Tyndale House Publishers, Wheaton, Illinois.

Scripture quotations designated NASB are from the *New American Standard Bible,* © 1960, 1962, 1963, 1968, 1971, 1972, 1973, 1975, 1977 by the Lockman Foundation, La Habra, California.

Any royalties from this book or the many other books by Bill Bright are dedicated to the glory of God and designated to the various ministries of Campus Crusade for Christ.

For more information, write:
L.I.F.E.—P. O. Box 40, Flemmington Markets, 2129, Australia
Campus Crusade for Christ of Canada—Box 300, Vancouver, B.C., V6C 2X3, Canada
Campus Crusade for Christ—Fairgate House, King's Road, Tyseley, Birmingham, B11 2AA, England
Lay Institute for Evangelism—P. O. Box 8786, Auckland 3, New Zealand
Campus Crusade for Christ—Alexandra, P. O. Box 0205, Singapore 9115, Singapore
Great Commission Movement of Nigeria—P. O. Box 500, Jos, Plateau State Nigeria, West Africa

Contents

Acknowledgments

Through the years, I have written many books and hundreds of articles. In the beginning years of my ministry, I personally researched, wrote, edited, and polished each book manuscript and article.

Today, however, my responsibilities of leading a large worldwide movement and my appointments and travel schedule do not allow me such luxury.

In need of help, I happily sought the assistance of my good friend and editor, Don Tanner, and his staff of NewLife Publications to help me revise this Leader's Guide to the *Five Steps of Christian Growth*.

A special thanks to Don for his professional assistance and to Joette Whims for joining Don and me in the editorial process.

A Personal Word

When I am alone with a person for a few minutes, I assume that I am there by divine appointment.

Shortly before midnight a few nights ago, a call came to my unlisted number. When the man on the line realized he had misdialed, he began to apologize. "I'm sorry, sir," he said, "I have a wrong number. I'm trying to call my wife. I dialed you by mistake."

"No," I quickly assured him. "It's no mistake. God has a message for you. Would you like to hear it?"

"Yes!" he replied.

I explained how much God loves him and that God has a wonderful plan for his life. We talked for a few more moments during which I learned that he and his wife were having marital difficulties. Finally, I asked, "Are you a Christian?"

"No."

"Would you like to be?"

"Oh, yes. My mother and brother are both Christians, and I have wanted to receive Christ for a long time."

"Do you know how to receive Jesus Christ as your Savior?"

"No, I don't."

I explained very simply how he could receive Christ, then suggested he pray with me—phrase by phrase—to invite Jesus into his life. After we finished praying, he expressed great gratitude and joy. Later, I rushed materials to him for assurance and spiritual growth and also arranged for personal follow-up.

After thousands of similar privileges, I am convinced of one thing: at least 50 percent of all non-believers in your "Jerusalem" and throughout the world would receive Christ if properly approached by a trained Spirit-filled believer who can communicate God's love and forgiveness revealed through our Lord Jesus Christ.

If you, too, have a deep desire to introduce others to Jesus, I encourage you to receive training in how to share your faith. And begin every day with a prayer like this:

> Lord, lead me to someone today whose heart You have prepared to receive the joyful news of our loving Savior. Enable me to be Your messenger to show others how to find forgiveness of sin and the gift of eternal life. Amen.

As you rise from your knees and go out into your world to study or work, the Holy Spirit will honor that simple, earnest prayer and guide you to those whom He has prepared for your witness. As you meet people in the course of your day, ask the Lord, "Is it he? Is it she? Where is the person You want me to introduce to You?"

Always carry a *Four Spiritual Laws* booklet or a similar presentation so that when the "divine appointment" occurs and you recognize the opportunity, you can aggressively share your faith. Whether or not they receive Christ, leave them with the *Gospel of John, A Man Without Equal* book, the *Four Spiritual Laws,* or something similar to read.

This *Five Steps of Christian Growth* study is designed to train you to grow as a disciple and to live a godly life so you can share your faith in Christ more effectively. You will learn how to lead even your first small group study. The helps for leaders on pages 9 through 20 will enable you to rel ax and lead with confidence. These easily understood lessons will help you prepare for leading the sessions. Special helps will dramatically reduce preparation time. You will discover how to:

- Prepare for the discussion
- Begin a sharing time
- Start and lead discussions

- Develop key ideas
- Help your students apply biblical principles to their lives

All you need is a desire to apply the biblical principles in these lessons to your life and a commitment to help others grow in Christ.

Leading a small group Bible study will be one of the richest, most meaningful, and most rewarding adventures of your lifetime. I encourage you to begin right now by asking the Lord who He would have you invite to join your group.

God will richly bless you for your obedience to His Word, and you will experience the reality of our Lord's promise to all who love and obey Him: "I will reveal myself to him" (John 14:21, TLB).

My prayer is that this study will bless and enrich your life and increase your effectiveness as a personal witness for our Lord. I assure you that there is no experience in life more exciting and spiritually rewarding than helping to introduce people to Christ.

Bill Bright

How to Lead a
Small Group Bible Study

Carl Sharsmith, an 81-year-old tour guide in California's Yosemite Park, had a deep love for nature. He and his "Smokey Bear" hat with the cracked-leather band had spent fifty years helping tourists discover the wonders of the spectacular park.

Today, his sunburned nose was dotted with flakes of white skin and his eyes were watery. He looked discouraged. He had heard once again the same old question he had heard repeatedly during his many years as a guide. A female tourist had rushed up to him and exclaimed, "I've got only an hour to spend at Yosemite. What should I do? Where should I go?"

The old naturalist replied with a sigh, "Ah, lady, only an hour." He paused and looked at the grandiose landscape all around them, then said, "I suppose that if I had only an hour to spend at Yosemite, I'd just walk over there by the river and sit down and cry."*

Maybe that's how you feel when you consider the content of the Bible and leading a Bible study. Perhaps you're thinking, *Leading a Bible study group scares me. How will I start the discussion? Will I have enough material? How can I help my group apply the biblical principles they are learning to their lives? How can I pass on to others the joy and excitement I feel in my relationship with God?*

That's why the *Five Steps of Christian Growth* curriculum was developed. This course of study is designed to give your students

---

*Adapted from "Yosemite—Forever?", *National Geographic Magazine*, National Geographic Society, Washington, D.C., January 1985, vol. 167, no. 1, p.55.

a broad survey of the Christian faith. They will learn of the wonderful privileges and responsibilities of the Christian life and discover the power of the Holy Spirit to transform the lives of men and women who trust and obey our Lord. And they will learn how to tap into the supernatural power of God for those life situations that require more than will power.

As a leader, you will help them grow and mature in Christ. To be a more effective leader, work at putting into practice the principles you will be teaching. It is not necessary to "master" each concept, or to feel that your performance in each area is perfect. It is essential, however, that you are growing in your relationship with Christ, in your walk in the Spirit, in the study of God's Word, and in sharing your faith with others.

Qualifications to Lead a Group

You do not need to be a theologian, Bible scholar, or great teacher. To be a leader:

- You should have previously, by faith, received Jesus Christ as your Savior and Lord.

- You should desire to know more about God and His truths as revealed in His holy Word, the Bible.

- You should desire to help others know Christ and learn these truths and be willing to devote time and effort to leading a group.

- You should avoid using controversial teachings that could cause confusion among group members.

If you meet these simple requirements, here is how to get started.

How to Start a Small Group Bible Study

Personal preparation is a vital first step. Be sure that Christ is Lord of your life and that you are filled with the Holy Spirit. I encourage you to read these booklets: the *Four Spiritual Laws* and *Have You Made the Wonderful Discovery of the Spirit-Filled*

Life? They contain the basic principles you will need to live a victorious Christian life and be an effective leader of your group. You can obtain them from your local Christian bookstore, your mail-order distributor, or New*Life* Publications.

Next, pray for God's leading and blessing. Then invite your friends or announce plans for your Bible study group to others at your job or in your dormitory or neighborhood. Often those to whom you have witnessed but who have not yet received Christ as Savior will be interested in participating in your group.

You can also show the video *A Man Without Equal* to neighbors, friends, or relatives and encourage those who receive Christ or who are interested in growing in their faith to participate in your group. The discussion on pages 21 through 26 will explain how to use the video.

New Christians and others who need spiritual follow-up are likely prospects for your group as well. Choose the people you think would be most interested, pray about them individually, then visit each one personally. After you make the contacts, select a meeting place and time for your Bible study.

Keep your group small. With eight to twelve people, group members will feel freer to interact and discuss the lesson material. You will also have more time to give your students individual attention as they begin to apply biblical truths in their lives.

Be sure your meeting place is neat, attractive, and well-ventilated. Choose a place where you will be free from interruption. If several days lapse between your initial contact and the first Bible study, remind those who have expressed interest. Make an announcement, speak to them personally, phone them, or send cards.

Avoid pressuring anyone to join your group. At the same time, do not have a negative or apologetic attitude. The best way to promote interest and enthusiasm is to be interested and enthusiastic yourself. Let me suggest some approaches.

"John, you've expressed an interest in knowing more about Christianity and the Bible. (Show him Lesson 1.) This has been a tremendous help to me in learning about the Bible in a short time. I think it could be a real help to both of us if we studied together."

or

"John, several of us are getting together to study the Bible. We believe that if we do it as a group, we will all benefit. Why don't you join us?"

As you pray and wait on God, He will lead you to those He has chosen for your study.

Your *Five Steps* Bible study group may be made up of Christians at different levels of spiritual maturity and possibly some who have not yet received Christ as their Savior. A few may already be familiar with some of the content while for others it will be completely new. The informal nature of a small group study is ideal for helping students learn from each other as well as from the things you say. Your Leader's Guide is carefully designed to help you guide the group's discovery of scriptural principles and to show how these truths can be applied to their lives.

Guidelines for Leading

Begin preparing for your group by thoroughly reading the following section of your Leader's Guide. To help you and your group get the most from the lessons, order a Study Guide for each member of your group and the resource materials that go along with each lesson. Listed at the beginning of each lesson under "Resources to Help You Lead the Study," the materials are available at your local Christian bookstore, your mail-order distributor, or New*Life* Publications.

When leading the sessions, follow these guidelines:

- Create an informal atmosphere so you and your group can get to know each other. Address each person by name. Introduce new members before the discussion begins. Contact visitors during the week and invite them to return for the next session. Pray daily for each person in your group.

- Have your Bible open at all times. If your students are unfamiliar with the Bible, offer to help them find Scripture verses and allow time for them to locate the passages in their own Bibles. If a student does not have a Bible, help him obtain one. The lesson material uses the *New International Version*. Bring extra Bibles and pencils for students to use during the study time.

- Be yourself. Depend on the Holy Spirit to work through the person you are, not through an artificial "spiritual leader" image that you would like to project.

- Don't be bound to your notes. Maintain eye contact with your group.

- A group leader is a discussion guide, not a lecturer. Rather than dominating the discussion, draw out comments from your students. Be prepared to suggest ideas, give background material, and ask questions to keep the conversation lively and relevant. If a student is saying something productive and to the point, refrain from inserting your own thoughts. When he finishes, guide, clarify, and summarize. Keep the discussion centered on the principle passages of Scripture. Encourage silent members of the group to get involved in the discussion.

- When you ask a question, allow time for students to think before continuing. Then listen to their answers rather than mentally planning what you are going to say next. Remember, you are teaching people, not lessons.

- Make sure everyone understands the major points in the lesson.

- Get involved in the lives of your group members. Communicating the basic truths of the Christian life is more than passing on information; it is sharing life experiences. Help them put into practice the truths you are teaching. The way you model and mentor through your personal example will have a far greater impact on your group than any of the words you say in a meeting.

Remember that each group has its own personality. Some groups are active, others more subdued. Adapt your leadership style to fit your group. But remember—your most important quality as a leader is to be open to the Holy Spirit's guidance as you help your students apply the lessons they are learning.

How to Encourage Participation

Your objective in all Bible studies is to encourage spiritual maturity among group members. Your main activity should be studying the Scriptures, and any discussion should follow the study outline in the lesson plan. To encourage participation, sit in a circle. Ideally, no group should have more than twelve people to avoid losing a feeling of intimacy. When your group exceeds that number, you may want to divide into two groups.

Here are some suggestions for encouraging members to participate and making the discussion time interesting and practical:

- Ask the group to read the Bible passage to be discussed, with each person reading one verse aloud. Invite one member to summarize the passage in his own words before asking any questions about it.

- When discussing the study questions, ask specific students to answer them. Avoid embarrassing anyone. When you ask a question of a member, be sure he answers it aptly. If he stumbles, help him along and make him feel that he did answer the question, at least in part. Compliment him on his response.

- If you sense confusion about a question you ask, restate it in different words or from another point of view.

- After one person has made a point, ask others if they agree. Have them state their reasons. Often a great deal can be learned by disagreeing over a passage. To keep the discussion from turning into an argument, remind everyone that you are studying what the Bible says about a specific subject.

- At the end of the discussion, have someone summarize the points that have been made. It is usually wise for the leader to guide the final summary and application.

- If a person asks a question that is off the topic, tactfully explain that it would be best not to take class time to discuss it. Offer to help answer the question personally after the study is over.

- Define all unusual words.

- Keep the discussion relevant and personal. Avoid arguments. Don't let one person dominate the discussion. To redirect the discussion, restate the question or ask for the answer to the next question.

- To stimulate discussion, ask such questions as: "What do you think this passage means?" "What can this passage teach us about God, Christ, ourselves, our responsibility, our relationships with others?"

- Help the students apply the passage personally. Ask, "What significance does this have for us today?" "What does this mean to you?" "How does (or will) it affect your life?"

- Keep the discussion moving. If you go through the material too quickly, the study will be shallow; if you go too slowly, it will seem tedious and boring. The lessons may include more material than you need. Don't spend too much time on any one section, but be sure you cover each major point. Be punctual about beginning and closing the session.

- Make the group time enjoyable. Allow extra time after the study for individual counseling, social interaction, and/or refreshments.

Objectives of the Five-Week Study

1. **Be sure that each person knows how to become a Christian.** Although you may have new believers in your group, you may also have worldly Christians (those who continually allow self rather than the Holy Spirit to control their lives) or non-Christians as well. In the first two lessons, emphasize the difference between someone simply knowing about the material studied and experiencing the principles personally in his life.

2. **Be sure that each believer knows he is a Christian.** Many people are unsure of their relationship with God. At the end of this five-week course, each person in your class should be able to clearly explain his personal commitment to Christ and understand that his salvation is because of his trust in Christ and not in any works he may do (Ephesians 2:8,9).

3. **Help each person begin growing in his Christian life.** While studying these five lessons, the members of your group will learn how to be sure of their salvation, how to experience God's love and forgiveness, how to be filled with the Holy Spirit and live a Spirit-filled life, and how to grow as a Christian.

How to Use the Lesson Plans

To teach this series of studies effectively, study each part of the lesson before the group session. *There is no substitute for preparation.* Studying the lesson thoroughly will enable you to lead the discussion with confidence. If you take shortcuts in your preparation time, it will be obvious to your group.

Prepare yourself for each session by doing the following:

- Pray for the individuals in the group. Compile a list of each person's special needs and refer to it during your personal prayer time.

- Thank God for what He will teach all of you.

- Reread the objectives of the study group.

- Study the resource materials that parallel the lesson you will be discussing. These books are listed under "Resources to Help You Lead the Study."

- Review the outline for the lesson.

- Study the verses and answers to the questions in each lesson. Since the answers are printed in your Leader's Guide, you may be tempted to skip this step. However, familiarity with the Scripture references and answers will help you during the group discussion.

Each lesson includes the following main parts:

Focus

This is a one-sentence summary of the subject covered in the lesson.

Objectives

These goals will help you keep the lesson on track. To help your students meet them, keep the goals in mind as you prepare the lesson and guide the discussion. A helpful technique is to jot the goals in your Leader's Guide where you want to emphasize them.

Session Scriptures

These verses will give you an overview of the material covered in the lesson. To prepare for group study, read them before class rather than in class.

Resources to Help You Lead the Study

Listed in some of the lessons are books, booklets, and video tapes that can help you guide your students through the lesson. Although the lesson is complete without these resources, they will help you better understand and teach the material. Check your local Christian bookstore or New*Life* Publications for these resources.

Outline

The outline presents the structure of the Bible study. Use it like you would a map to help you see where you are going.

Leader's Preparation

This material is for your enrichment and instruction in presenting the lesson. It also gives you guidelines on what to bring to the session and information on how to guide the study. Review this section just before you come to class.

The Bible Study Session

Your Leader's Guide is organized to help you guide the study. The following techniques show how the material in the Leader's Guide Bible Study Session is to be used:

- The directions for the leader are in bold.

- The answers to questions are in parentheses and italicized.

- Have members fill out their books during the study.

Sharing

This opening time is designed to help your group share progress in applying last week's lesson. Relate personal joys and concerns as well as experiences that you or other members of your group have had. Set a friendly, non-threatening tone for the discussion time. Before beginning the lesson, open with prayer asking the Holy Spirit to guide the study and open your hearts to God's Word.

Discussion Starter

Your opening question and the resulting discussion should stimulate thinking but not necessarily supply answers. Guide the discussion by interjecting further questions. Do not correct wrong answers at this time, but use them to stimulate thinking.

Lesson Development

This section gives the directions for leading the Bible study. The ideas will help you vary your presentation, involve each person, and help group members understand each principle studied. Adapt the teaching suggestions to your group size and personalities and to your leadership style. When reading Scripture passages, use different methods. For example:

- Read the passage aloud while the group follows along.

- Have everyone read it silently.

- Ask a different person to read each paragraph or each verse.

- Ask one of the better readers to read while others follow along.

Application

This section will help you challenge your group members to apply what they have learned. Many of the application questions should be answered by each member privately. Your role is to guide their thinking and lead them to personal decisions.

Closing and Prayer

This part of the lesson will help you lead your students to use the applications in the lesson. Discuss questions or material as necessary, then you or one of the members lead the group in prayer. Also use this time to pray for specific needs and concerns expressed by your group members.

Follow-up

This section will remind you to pray for your group members and will tell you when to contact them between lessons. It will also help you prepare for the next week's lesson.

Student Lesson Plan

Located at the end of each lesson, this plan is duplicated in the Study Guide. Instructions in the Leader's Guide tell you when to use the Study Guide material. The students should fill out their books during group time.

As you begin studying these lessons, God will open your mind and heart to the truths presented here. I am confident that your learning and your teaching will result in spiritual growth, an abundant life, and a fruitful ministry for you and those whom you touch for Jesus Christ. It will be one of the most rewarding experiences of your life.

A Man Without Equal
Video Presentation

One of the most effective ways to introduce others to Jesus and to help believers grow and mature in their Christian faith is to show the thirty-minute video *A Man Without Equal*.* Showing this video in advance to different individuals and groups can help you begin your *Five Steps* Bible study. Schedule several showings and invite those who respond to the message in the video to join the five-week Bible study. Here are some suggestions on ways you can use the video:

- Have a video party in your dorm room or student lounge.

- Plan a showing to your fraternity or sorority.

- Present the video to an athletic team.

- Show the video to your Sunday school class or during an evening church service.

- Use it during a retreat.

- Invite friends and neighbors into your home for a special showing.

- Present the video during the lunch hour or another appropriate time at your job.

- Arrange showings to service men or women in your military unit.

---

*You can also use the "JESUS" video to present the message of God's love and forgiveness. This video shows the life of Jesus as found in the Gospel of Luke and gives the viewer an opportunity to receive Christ as Savior and Lord. For more information on this video, write to: New*Life* Publications, 100 Sunport Lane, Orlando, FL 32809.

- Use it as part of your prison ministry.

- Show the video to your civic group.

- Give a video to individuals whom you are seeking to introduce to Christ, and arrange a follow-up appointment.

Prepare for your video showing by making a list of those you plan to invite. Pray for each one, asking God to prepare their hearts.

Choose the place for the meeting. You will need the location one to two hours, depending on whether you serve refreshments. Your home would be an excellent informal setting. For a larger group, consider renting a meeting room in an apartment complex, public library, or other facility. Perhaps your employer has a meeting room you can reserve.

Then decide whether you will provide refreshments. They should be simple and easy to serve so you can concentrate on the presentation. You could ask a Christian friend to act as the host and arrange for the food.

Begin inviting people two or three weeks before the presentation. If appropriate, send invitations. Those you contact are more likely to remember and respond to a written invitation than word-of-mouth or a telephone call. Mention in the invitation that you are showing a video about Jesus called *A Man Without Equal.* List the date, time, and place of the meeting. Include your phone number so people can let you know whether they will attend, ask questions about the meeting, or leave your number with a babysitter. If you are serving refreshments, mention that, too.

The number of guests you invite will vary with your situation. If you know everyone on your prospective guest list quite well, send about twice as many invitations as you want guests at the presentation. If you do not know your potential guests, you may need to send six times as many invitations.

Two to three days before the meeting, call each person on your list. This can dramatically increase attendance, and allow you to answer any concerns or questions they may have about the event.

Prepare your materials in advance. You will need the following:

- A television set
- A VCR
- *A Man Without Equal* video
- The discussion card that comes with the video
- Blank 3×5 cards
- Pens or pencils
- A *Four Spiritual Laws* booklet for each person attending

The day of the video showing, arrange the meeting room so everyone will have a good view of the TV screen. Put your materials on the most centrally located table or chair so you can guide the discussion after the presentation. Greet your guests warmly as they arrive. Put them at ease and create a friendly atmosphere. Ask your guests about their families, jobs, schools, or other personal interests. Discuss current events from the newspaper, radio, or TV, or talk about a good book that you have read. Avoid discussing your church or Christian subjects that might offend a non-Christian.

When it is time to begin the meeting, ask your guests to find a seat. Thank your host and give the reason for the showing. Keep your comments to just a couple of minutes. Then explain that you will be handing out cards for each of them to write down their comments following the video.

Here is an example of what you could say:

Before we see the video, I want to thank Brian for providing refreshments. Both he and I are excited about what Jesus has been doing in our lives. That is why we have asked all of you to see this video. It shows who Jesus is and how He has changed the course of history.

After we have seen the video, we'll have a short discussion time. Then, I would like each of you to comment on the video and

this evening's discussion. When we finish, we'll have something
to eat and spend time getting to know each other.

I'm going to start the video now. I'm sure you will find it
challenging.

Dim the lights and start the video. At the conclusion of the
video, give a *Four Spiritual Laws* booklet to each person and
discuss questions 1 through 5 from the "Questions for Reflection
and Discussion" that accompany the video. The following are
sample responses to the questions:

1. What was Jesus' greatest teaching? (Mark 16:16; John 3:16–
   18) *(That salvation is by faith, not works. According to Romans 3:23, all of us have sinned and do not measure up to
   God's standards. Sin is going our way independent of God.
   Jesus died on the cross to pay the penalty for our sins. He came
   to reconcile us to God.)*

   Why was this teaching so unique? *(All other major religions
   teach that we must work our way to God.)*

   What does this teaching mean in your life? *(It means that I
   can have a relationship with God without first having to make
   myself acceptable to Him.)*

2. Give several examples of how Jesus' influence on people
   and nations has altered the course of history, your country,
   your city, your neighborhood. *(Allow guests to discuss each
   of these points freely. Some examples are that our laws are
   based on teachings in the New Testament. Social changes such
   as labor laws, the abolition of slavery, social work, and the rise
   of the status of women began when godly Christians started
   working to right those wrongs. Hospitals and hospices started
   in the Middle Ages to follow Jesus' example of compassion for
   the sick and needy. Modern science was founded on the Christian concept of an orderly universe.)*

3. What are people in your circle of influence saying about
   Jesus? What are some of the doubts you have felt about
   Jesus either in the past or in the present? *(Allow guests to*

give their opinions on both these questions. Be sensitive to those who still question what Jesus means to them.)

4. What personal feelings about Jesus were confirmed as you watched the video? *(Begin the discussion by giving your feelings. Then let others respond.)*

5. Jesus claimed to be the Son of God and the Savior of mankind. After viewing the video, who do you believe He is? *(Jesus is the Son of God and my Savior.)*

   How would you explain this to others? *(Let others give their ideas.)*

Pass out the 3×5 cards and pencils. Ask the viewers to write their names, addresses, and telephone numbers on one side of the card. On the other side, ask them to:

1. Write brief answers to these questions:

   - Have you received Jesus as your Savior and Lord? When?

   - Are you interested in learning more about how Jesus can change your life?

     Describe the five-week Bible study that you will be starting. Explain that you will contact them later about the time and place for your first meeting.

2. Write specific comments about the video and the discussion.

If some in your group are Christians who are growing in their relationship to Christ, challenge them with question 6 from "Questions for Reflection and Discussion." If most are not believers or have just made a decision to follow Christ, skip this question and invite all those who have viewed the video to join your upcoming Bible study.

Thank your guests for coming and explain that you will be available for any questions during the refreshment time. Then dismiss your group with a prayer similar to this one:

Dear Jesus,

Thank You for Your presence here in this meeting. Thank You for dying on the cross and paying for each of our sins. Help each person make a decision to receive You into his or her life. Help us serve You. Amen.

Collect the cards and serve the refreshments. While others are chatting and eating, be available to talk with anyone who may want to receive Christ as Savior or who has questions. If someone is unsure of how to receive Christ, go through the *Four Spiritual Laws* booklet with him.

After your guests leave, look over the 3×5 cards and plan when you can contact each person. Prayerfully do so over the next few days if at all possible. Encourage each one to come to your *Five Steps* Bible study.

LESSON 1

How You Can Be Sure You Are a Christian

Focus

A person can be sure he is a Christian when he decides by faith to trust in Christ as his Savior and Lord; this decision involves the intellect, the emotions, and the will.

Objectives

This session will help students to:

- *Understand* the importance of the intellect, emotions, and will in making a commitment to Christ

- *Identify* the basis of their own personal commitment to Christ

Session Scriptures

John 10:30–33; John 14:6–9; Ephesians 2:8–10

Resources to Help You Lead the Study

- Transferable Concept: *How You Can Be Sure You Are a Christian*

- *Ten Basic Steps Toward Christian Maturity: The Christian Adventure*

Outline

    I. The new birth
   II. Intellectual commitment
  III. Emotional commitment

IV. Commitment of the will
V. The basis of your relationship with Christ
VI. Our confidence in Christ
VII. God's promises to all Christians

Leader's Preparation

Use Lesson 1 as an opportunity to share the gospel with those who have not received Christ or surrendered their lives to His lordship. Bring a copy of the *Four Spiritual Laws* for each person in your group. For your reference, the booklet has been reproduced on pages 105 through 108. You can purchase the booklets at your local Christian bookstore.

If you have never shared the *Four Spiritual Laws* with a non-Christian, practice leading someone to Christ by reading through the booklet with a friend before your first group meeting.

Review the material under "How to Lead a Small Group Bible Study" on pages 9 through 20. Following is some additional background information on the Session Scriptures to help you discuss the material confidently.

John 10:30–33. In the context of John 10:22–39, Jesus was confronted by Jewish religious leaders over His claim to be the Messiah (the promised Savior predicted in Old Testament writings). Jesus says these leaders are not willing to believe in Him, therefore anything He says or does will not convince them of who He is.

The conclusion of Jesus' argument is a challenge: "Don't believe me unless I do miracles of God. But if I do, believe them even if you don't believe me. Then you will become convinced that the Father is in me, and I in the Father" (verses 37,38, TLB).

John 14:6–9. This passage is also part of a larger context (verses 1–14). In verse 8, Philip asked Jesus, "Lord, show us the Father." Jesus appeals to His miracles as evidence for His claims of deity. Jesus deals with the mystery of the relationship between Himself and the Father. While some students may want to debate this concept, keep your group's attention focused on the divinity of Jesus. Another passage that deals with the deity of Christ is Philippians 2:5–11.

Ephesians 2:8–10. Take a few moments to read the first ten verses of this chapter. Paul vividly describes the contrast between the Christian's condition now and before he was changed by Christ. From spiritual death, the Christian has moved into abundant (joyful, fruitful, Spirit-filled) life. No corpse can bring itself back to life. Nor can anyone generate spiritual life by human effort. God alone is the source of this life, and He bestows it as a free gift.

The Transferable Concept: *How You Can Be Sure You Are a Christian* expands the message in this lesson. Read it thoroughly to help you lead this study.

Arrange chairs and set out the Study Guides, extra Bibles, and pencils in preparation for the meeting. Greet each person as he or she arrives. Make sure everyone has a Bible. (It may help group members find references more quickly if they use the *New International Version.*) Have available a flip chart or large sheet of paper, 3×5 cards, a small sheet of paper for each student, pencils, extra Bibles, and Study Guides.

The Bible Study Session

Remember these directions for using this lesson:

- **The leader's directions are in bold type.**

- **The answers to questions are in parentheses and italicized.**

- **Have members fill out their books during the study.**

Sharing (5–10 minutes)

As new members arrive, give them a Study Guide and ask them to complete a 3×5 card. Have them write their names, addresses, and phone numbers on one side of the card and write brief answers to these two questions on the other side: Have you received Jesus as your Savior and

Lord? If so, when? Add the new cards to the ones you already have so you will have a record of those attending your Bible study.

Ask the group members to state their names. Explain that you are there to guide the sessions. The Bible will be the authority, not you. Stating this at the beginning will take some pressure off your role as leader.

Discussion Starter (8–10 minutes)

Ask: How is our association with Christ similar to a marriage relationship? **Ask the students to identify qualities that help a marriage relationship grow. Emphasize the importance of committing your intellect, emotions, and will to your marriage partner. Help students describe what happens in a marriage when one of these elements is missing. Then do the same with a commitment to Christ.**

Explain that the first part of the study will focus on the commitment of our intellect, emotions, and will to Christ.

Lesson Development (30–40 minutes)

The New Birth

Begin by saying: Jesus tells us what we must do to receive eternal life. Let us look at what He said to a man who came to Him for counsel. **Turn to the third chapter of John's Gospel and read the first eight verses.**

Explain: We become Christians through a spiritual birth. God is Spirit and without His indwelling presence, we cannot communicate with Him. Consider an example of a caterpillar crawling in the dust. One day this ugly, hairy worm weaves a cocoon around its body. From this cocoon emerges a beautiful butterfly.

We do not understand fully what takes place. We realize only that where once a worm crawled in the dust, now a butterfly soars through the air. A similar transformation takes place in our lives as we experience the new birth. Where once we lived on the lowest level as sinful, egocentric individuals, we can now dwell on the highest plane, experiencing full and abundant (joyful, fruitful, Spirit-filled) lives as children of God, if we trust and obey Him.

Becoming a Christian involves a commitment to Him of your intellect, emotions, and will. Let's examine, one by one, each of these elements of the new birth. **Go through "The New Birth" in the Student Lesson Plan.**

Intellectual Commitment

Ask half your group to read John 10:30–33 while the others read John 14:6–9, and then answer the question in the Study Guide. After three or four minutes, ask the groups to share the claims of Jesus that they discovered.

Look up each verse and discuss what each person thought of Jesus:

1. The apostle John. John 1:1,14 *(John said that the Word is God and that Jesus is the Word. Therefore, Jesus is God.)*

2. Thomas. John 20:25–28 *(Thomas called Jesus his God, and Jesus accepted the title.)*

3. Jesus' enemies. John 5:18 *(His enemies tried to kill Jesus because He claimed to be God.)*

Read Romans 1:3,4. Ask: What is the ultimate proof of Christ's claim to be God? *(The resurrection.)* According to verses 5,6,16,17 of Romans 1, how does the proof of Christ's power affect your life? *(We obey Him; we experience grace and peace; we are not ashamed of the gospel; and we live by faith.)* **Discuss how each promise we received affects our new life.**

To help students see that Jesus claimed to be God, go through this Trilemma Chart. Draw it on a flip chart or large piece of paper as you go through each point.

Trilemma Posed by the Claims of Christ

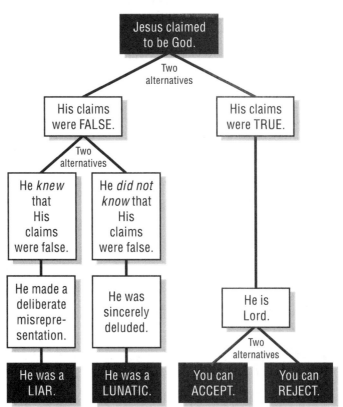

Ask: As you look at this chart, how did your thinking change about the claims Christ made? **Allow several students to answer.**

At this point, be sensitive about whether everyone understands who Jesus is. Then read: Jesus of Nazareth was conceived by the Holy Spirit and was born of the virgin Mary almost 2,000 years ago. Hundreds of years before, the great prophets of Israel foretold His coming. The Old Testament, which was written by many individuals over a period of 1,500 years, contains more than 300 references to His coming.

At the age of thirty, Jesus began His public ministry. In the three years that followed, He taught His disciples how to receive eternal life and how to live an abundant life on this earth.

The life that Jesus led, the miracles He performed, the words He spoke, His death on the cross, His resurrection, His ascent to heaven all point to the fact that He was more than a mere man. What do the following verses tell us about who Jesus is and what He did for us?

Ask the following questions, allowing about five minutes of silence for students to write the answers in their books. Then go over each question aloud.

1. Why did Jesus have to come to this earth? Romans 3:23 *(Because we have all sinned and are separated from God.)*

2. Why did Jesus die for us? 1 Peter 3:18 *(He died to bring us into a right relationship with God.)*

3. What has Jesus Christ done for our sins that no one else can do? 1 Peter 2:24,25 *(He took our sins upon Himself so that we might receive forgiveness from God and live a life of righteousness.)*

4. Why is Christ's resurrection from the dead significant to us? 1 Peter 1:3 *(Because Christ rose from the dead, we can know that His promise of eternal life is sure.)*

Emotional Commitment

Read: An emotional feeling or reaction to a specific act, event, or experience can be different for different people, including the moment we received Christ as Savior and Lord. The failure to distinguish between different types of emotions has caused many people to become confused in their relationship with God. **Give the students time to find the next two answers:**

1. What kind of experience did Paul have when he first met Jesus? Acts 22:6–10 *(A dramatic experience.)*

2. What was Timothy's experience? 2 Timothy 1:5 *(A quiet experience through the instruction of godly parents.)*

Say: Emotions are a normal part of life. Different emotions cause us to respond to God differently. One person may have a highly emotional personality; another may be calm and reserved. Because emotions vary greatly, we should not depend upon them. An emphasis on emotions is probably the one thing that has caused more people to lack the assurance of a relationship with God through Jesus. Seeking an emotional experience contradicts Hebrews 11:6. **Read the verse.**

Say: Faith is another word for trust. This trust must be placed in God and His Word rather than in what we feel.

Refer to the train diagram and show how faith, not feelings, should control our lives.

- Fact: The facts about the Christian life are in the Bible. Does a fact change? *(No.)*

- Faith: If we put faith in our feelings and our feelings change with our circumstances, what will our faith do? *(Vary up and down.)* If we put our faith in facts, what will our faith be like? *(Stable and sure.)*

- Feelings: Do our feelings change? *(Yes.)*

Ask: In what situations do Christians tend to trust in feelings rather than in God's Word? *(Some answers could be: spending money, facing conflict or pressure, or handling a tense situation while driving a car.)* **Describe a time when you trusted God rather than feelings. Speculate on what might have happened if you had followed your emotions instead.**

Ask: How can you let your faith control these situations? List specific ways you plan to do this. **If a group member begins**

using another person as an example, gently lead the discussion back to situations he or she faces personally.

Commitment of the Will

Say: A commitment to Christ involves an act of the will. Although both mind and feelings are valid, you are not a Christian until, as an act of your will, you make a decision to receive Christ as your Savior and Lord.

Relating the commitment of marriage to that of receiving Christ as Savior, ask: Have you taken this step? When? **Encourage each person to write his answers in his Study Guide.**

Discuss how these three elements of commitment—fact, faith, feelings—interact to enable us to make the right decisions.

Allow the students time to fill in questions 1 through 4 in their books.

The following are facts in which you can place your faith:

1. Christ came into your life. Revelation 3:20.

   ■ What does the door refer to? *(My heart.)*

   ■ What does Christ promise? *(To come in.)*

   ■ What is our part? *(To open the door.)*

   ■ What is His part? *(To come in.)*

   ■ According to this verse, if you by faith open the door of your heart and invite Jesus Christ to come into your life to be your Savior and Lord, will He come in? *(Yes.)*

2. Your sins were forgiven. Colossians 1:14.

   ■ How many of your sins were forgiven? *(All of them.)*

   ■ If God has forgiven you, why are there times when you are haunted by guilt feelings? 1 John 1:8,9 *(Because of unconfessed sin in my life.)*

- What can be done about unconfessed sin? *(Confess it to God.)*

3. You became a child of God. John 1:12,13.

- Who has been spiritually born into God's family? *(Those who have received Christ.)*

- When you received Christ, what did you become? *(A child of God.)*

4. You received eternal life. 1 John 5:11–13.

- According to this passage, who is the only One who can give us eternal life? *(Christ.)*

- Verse 13 says, "I write these things to you who believe in the name of the Son of God so that you may know that you have eternal life." According to Hebrews 13:5, if you have eternal life now, will it ever be taken away from you? *(No.)*

The Basis of Your Relationship with Christ

Have the students read these verses and answer the questions from the Student Lesson Plan: According to 1 Corinthians 15:1–4, what is the message of the gospel? *(Christ died for our sins, was buried, and rose again.)* According to 1 Corinthians 15:3 and Hebrews 9:22, why did Christ have to die? *(Without the shedding of blood, sins can't be forgiven.)* According to John 1:12, what happens when a person responds to the gospel and receives Christ into his life? *(He becomes a child of God.)*

Our Confidence in Christ

Read Ephesians 2:8,9 and review how a person becomes a Christian. Have the students fill out this section in their books, then ask:

- What is grace? *(Unmerited favor from God)*

- In what are we to have faith? Compare Galatians 3:22,26. *(Jesus Christ)*

- On what basis did you obtain it? *(Faith.)*

- How do good works relate to your salvation? *(Salvation is received through faith, not through works.)*

- Why is boasting not acceptable? *(Because we did not save ourselves.)*

Ask: Do you have the assurance that Christ is in your life? Are you sure that if you died right now, you would spend eternity with God in heaven? **Let students answer voluntarily.** If you cannot answer yes, make certain of your salvation by receiving Christ by a definite, deliberate act of your will right now in prayer. Here is a prayer you can use:

> Lord Jesus, I need You. Thank You for dying on the cross for my sins. I open the door of my life and receive You as my Savior and Lord. Thank You for forgiving my sins and giving me eternal life. Make me the kind of person You want me to be. Amen.

Ask: If you have invited Christ into your life, now or earlier, where is He right now? *(In my heart and life.)* By what authority do you know this? *(The promise of God in His Word.)*

Instruct: Rewrite Ephesians 2:8,9 in words you would use to explain them to a friend. **Give students time to complete this, then ask them to share what they wrote with the group.**

God's Promises to All Christians

Ask: What do these verses promise you as a result of your decision to trust in Christ? **Allow time for members to write their answers, then go over each as a group.**

- Revelation 3:20 *(Christ will come into your life.)*

- 1 John 5:11–13 *(We receive eternal life.)*

- John 10:27–29 *(No one can take us away from the Father.)*

- John 5:24 *(We pass from death into life.)*

Ask: Which promise is most meaningful to you? Why? **Allow several students to answer.**

Ask: How can you apply these verses to strengthen your faith?

As a result of what we have discussed, how can a person be sure of personal salvation? *(God has promised in His holy Word that no person or situation can take these things away from us. Romans 8:35–39.)*

Application (8 minutes)

Distribute a small sheet of paper to each person. Ask them to write their name on the page and answer this question: "How do you know you have a relationship with Christ?" Go over the Action Point at the end of the Student Lesson. State that the group will be sharing these experiences during the next study.

Collect the sheets. Use this information to assess how well students understand the meaning of a personal relationship with Christ. Before next week, contact any student who feels unsure of his salvation.

Closing and Prayer (5 minutes)

Mention that the following week's study will cover how we can have constant communication with our heavenly Father. Close with a short prayer thanking God for His great love and sacrifice for us.

Follow-up

Group members will probably begin to express some needs in their lives. Discreetly jot them down on the member's 3×5 card as needs are mentioned. After the group leaves, record on each person's card their answer from the sheet of paper. Pray for these needs during the week.

Begin meeting with each member of your group after the study to build a good relationship. Share what God is currently teaching you. Your group members need to see you as a fellow learner, not as one who "has all the answers."

Student Lesson Plan

The New Birth

Receiving Jesus Christ as Savior means experiencing a new, spiritual birth. Read John 3:1–8 and write a description of this new birth.

Our relationship with Christ involves three areas of commitment: intellect, emotions, and will. Which area creates the most problems for you?

Intellectual Commitment

Christianity is not a "blind" leap of faith, but a personal relationship with God through Jesus Christ. Read John 10:30–33 and 14:6–9.

How does Jesus' claim to be one with the Father ensure His ability to forgive sins?

What did each of the following people think about Jesus?

1. The apostle John (John 1:1,14)

2. Thomas (John 20:25–28)

3. Jesus' enemies (John 5:18)

According to Romans 1:3,4, what is the ultimate proof of Christ's claim to be God? How does this affect your life (verses 5,6,16,17)?

The life that Jesus led, the miracles He performed, the words He spoke, His death on the cross, His resurrection, and His ascent to heaven all point to the fact that He was more than a mere man. What do the following verses tell us about who Jesus is and what He did for us?

1. Why did Jesus have to come to this earth? (Romans 3:23)

2. Why did Jesus die for us? (1 Peter 3:18)

3. What has Jesus Christ done for our sins that no one else can do? (1 Peter 2:24,25)

4. Why is Christ's resurrection from the dead significant to us? (1 Peter 1:3)

Emotional Commitment

Seeking an emotional experience contradicts Hebrews 11:6. Faith is another word for trust. This trust must be placed in God and His Word rather than in what we feel. In what situations do you tend to trust in feelings rather than in God's Word?

1. What kind of experience did Paul have when he first met Jesus? (Acts 22:6–10)

2. What was Timothy's experience? (2 Timothy 1:5)

This diagram shows how we should let faith control our lives.

How can you let your faith control these situations? List specific ways you plan to do this.

Commitment of the Will

A commitment to Christ involves an act of the will. Although both mind and feelings are valid, you are not a Christian until, as an act of your will, you make a decision to receive Christ as your Savior and Lord. Have you taken this step? When?

The following are facts in which you can place your faith:

1. Christ came into your life. (Revelation 3:20)

- What does the door refer to?

- What does Christ promise?

- What is our part?

- What is His part?

- According to this verse, if you by faith open the door of your heart and invite Jesus Christ to come into your life to be your Savior and Lord, will He come in?

2. Your sins were forgiven. (Colossians 1:14)

- How many of your sins were forgiven?

- If God has forgiven you, why are there times when you are haunted by guilt feelings? (1 John 1:8,9)

- What can be done about unconfessed sin?

3. You became a child of God. (John 1:12,13)

- Who has been spiritually born into God's family?

- When you received Christ, what did you become?

4. You received eternal life. (1 John 5:11–13)

- According to this passage, who is the only One who can give us eternal life?

- Verse 13 says, "I write these things to you who believe in the name of the Son of God so that you may know that you have eternal life." According to Hebrews 13:5, if you have eternal life now, will it ever be taken away from you?

The Basis of Your Relationship with Christ

- What is the message of the gospel? (1 Corinthians 15:1–4)

- Why did Christ have to die? (1 Corinthians 15:3; Hebrews 9:22)

- What happens when a person responds to the gospel and receives Christ into his life? (John 1:12)

Our Confidence in Christ

If our relationship with God were dependent on our own good works, we could never have assurance of salvation. Read Ephesians 2:8,9 and answer these questions:

- What is grace?

- In what are we to have faith? (See Galatians 3:22,26.)

- On what basis did you obtain it?

- How do good works relate to your salvation?

- Why is boasting not acceptable?

Rewrite Ephesians 2:8,9 and Galatians 3:22–26 in words you would use to explain the verses to a friend.

God's Promises to All Christians

What do these verses promise you as a result of your decision to trust in Christ?

- Revelation 3:20

- 1 John 5:11–13

- John 10:27–29

- John 5:24

Which promise is most meaningful to you? Why?

How can you apply these verses to strengthen your faith?

Action Point: This coming week, explain to a friend why you are sure you are a Christian.

LESSON

2

How You Can Experience God's Love and Forgiveness

Focus

A Christian must confess his sins to experience God's love and forgiveness.

Objectives

This session will help students to:

- *Understand* the three types of people described in 1 Corinthians 2:14–3:3

- *Identify and handle* false guilt

- *Understand* "exhaling" in the concept of "Spiritual Breathing"

- *Apply* "exhaling" (confession) in their lives

Session Scriptures

Romans 7:25–8:11; 1 Corinthians 2:14–3:3; Hebrews 10:1–4, 10–18; 1 John 1:9; Psalm 32:1–5

Resources to Help You Lead the Study

- Transferable Concept: *How You Can Experience God's Love and Forgiveness*

Outline

I. Three types of people
   A. Natural person
   B. Spiritual person
   C. Worldly person

II. Spiritual Breathing
III. Handling guilt

Leader's Preparation

Study the material in Lessons 2 and 3 that explains "Spiritual Breathing" to familiarize yourself with the content. Practice Spiritual Breathing before teaching your students how to apply it in their lives. The Bible study sections most likely to raise questions among your students are 1 Corinthians 2:14–3:3 and Hebrews 10:1–4,10–18. The following information will help you answer some basic questions.

1 Corinthians 2:14–3:3. Paul is writing to a group of Christians beset by divisions and sin because they were carrying over values and attitudes from their old lives into their Christian experiences. Paul wants them see that there is more to the Christian life than the initial decision to receive Christ.

Paul distinguishes between the things of the world and things of the Spirit. Many people find it difficult to accept biblical truth because spiritual things are not reasoned through natural thought processes. Even those who have Christ in their lives find it hard to accept some truths if they have not yielded themselves to Christ's control. This does not mean that yielding to Christ requires abandoning rational thought. Instead, it involves using our God-given ability to think as originally intended, free of the bias of sin and selfish desire.

Hebrews 10:1–4,10–18. The Old Testament system of offering sacrifices for sin seems foreign to us today. Many people believe that killing animals to deal with human sin was brutal, barbaric, and superstitious. This system, however, accomplished several significant things:

- *God communicated the seriousness and high cost of sin.* To an agrarian society dependent on animal herds for survival, the sacrifice of a lamb or ox vividly underscored this point.

- *God chose the shedding of blood as the means by which people could experience cleansing from sin.* Furthermore, the sacrifices were an objective act that helped people believe God would forgive.

- *The animal sacrifices foreshadowed Jesus Christ's sacrificial death* on the cross for our sins.

The Transferable Concept: *How You Can Experience God's Love and Forgiveness* expands the message in this lesson. Read it thoroughly to help you lead the study.

The Bible Study Session

Remember these directions for using this lesson:

- **The leader's directions are in bold type.**

- **The answers to questions are in parentheses and italicized.**

- **Have members fill out their books during the study.**

Sharing (5 minutes)

Take a few moments to share experiences from the Action Point in Lesson 1. Ask: How did it affect you to explain to someone how you can be sure you are a Christian? How did it affect your friend?

Discussion Starter (8–10 minutes)

Read John 10:10. Discuss: Jesus intended the Christian life to be an exciting, abundant adventure. But most Christians do not know anything about this type of life. To many, the Christian life is a burden, a chore, a terrible cross to bear. They have never experienced the victory that Christ can give. Why do many Christians fail to experience this abundant life? **Allow students to respond.**

Lesson Development (30–40 minutes)

The Problem of Sin

Say: All of us face daily struggles with temptation and sin. But what is sin? Most people think of a list of don'ts when they think of sin. Paul, however, writes in Romans 14:23, "Everything that does not come from faith is sin."

The word "faith" in the Bible means to "trust in, rely upon." Sin, then, is not a matter of lying, cheating, being immoral, or any other act. These are only the results of an attitude of sin. Sin, rather, is any lack of conformity to the will of God, anything we do that does not come from our trust or reliance on God. Attitudes such as worry, irritability, and depression are symptoms of our lack of trust in God. Therefore, a good definition of sin is doing what *we* want instead of what *God* wants—both in attitude and action.

Ask: What does the Scripture say about sin? **Read each verse and discuss the answer. Encourage members to write answers in their books.**

1. Who has sinned? Romans 3:23 *(Every person on earth.)*

2. How did the sin of Adam, the father of the human race, affect you? Romans 5:12 *(I inherited my sin nature through Adam's sin.)*

3. What is the difference between temptation and sin?

   - Who is the tempter? Matthew 4:1 *(Satan.)*

   - What causes you to be drawn into temptation? James 1:13–15 *(My own evil thoughts and wishes.)*

   - How does sin differ from temptation? *(Temptation is the initial impression that may lead to sin.)*

Discuss: Why do we sin? **Read Romans 8:7,8.** *(Every member of the human race is born with an old sin nature, inherited from Adam's disobedience. Therefore we are all slaves to sin. We are by* *nature degenerate and corrupt. We are not sinners because we sin but we sin because we are sinners. Only through Christ's death on the cross can we be free from the penalty and power of sin.)*

What Is the Basis for Our Forgiveness?

Explain: If you are a Christian, you don't have to carry the guilt of sin. Your sins have been forgiven. Jesus' sacrifice for our sins was perfect in God's sight. We cannot add anything to what Christ has already done. We simply accept His forgiveness and cleansing by faith.

Read the following questions and write down the answers in the Study Guide.

1. According to John 1:29, what is Jesus called and what does He do? *(The Lamb of God; He takes away sin.)*

Read Hebrews 10:1–18.

2. What did Jesus do for our sins? *(He gave Himself to God as a sacrifice for our sins.)*

   Was this acceptable to God? *(Yes.)*

3. What did the sacrifice of Jesus accomplish for us? *(We received forgiveness of our sins and perfection in the sight of God.)*

4. How many of your sins did Christ forgive? *(All of them.)*

The Power of Sin

Say: According to Romans 6:1–18, Christ not only died for our sin and forgave it, He also delivered us from sin's power. **Read the verses. Say:** In these verses, Paul describes how the Christian is identified with Jesus Christ in His death, burial, and resurrection. When Christ died, we died. When He rose, we rose with Him. So, just as Christ conquered the power of sin with His death and resurrection, He also struck a death blow to our old sin nature—that part of us that loves to sin.

Answer the following questions.

1. What does God's Word tell you happened to your old sin nature when you became a Christian? *(It was crucified—killed.)*

2. According to verse 11, what must you do? *(I must consider my old sin nature dead and be alive to God.)*

3. According to verses 16 and 17, what choice faces you continuously? *(To serve sin or to serve God.)*

4. What limit does God place on the temptations you face? 1 Corinthians 10:13 *(They will not overpower me.)*

5. What does God promise to provide you with when you are tempted? *(A way to escape.)*

Say: We are to consider our old sin nature as dead—as an act of our will by faith. The control that sin had over us before we were Christians has been destroyed by Christ through His death and resurrection. As we go about our daily life, however, we are constantly tempted to yield to the desires of our old sin nature. When we are tempted, we have a choice. We can obey sin or obey God and find victory over temptation.

Three Types of People

Say: Christians who have not surrendered every area of their lives to God can become part of the problem in our society rather than the solution. The Bible explains why this is true by describing three types of people in the world. **Read 1 Corinthians 2:14–3:3. Using the Student Lesson Plan and the rest of this section in your Leader's Guide, explain the diagrams, read the verses for each diagram, and underline the answers as a group.**

The *natural person* is not a Christian (1 Corinthians 2:14). What are the qualities in his life?

Self-Directed Life

S – Self is on the throne

✝ – Christ is outside the life

● – Interests are directed by self, often resulting in discord and frustration

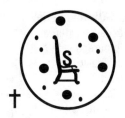

- *(He depends solely upon his own resources.)*

- *(Spiritually, he is dead to God—separated from God by sin.)*

The *spiritual person* is a Christian controlled and empowered by God's Spirit, called the Holy Spirit (1 Corinthians 2:15,16).

Christ-Directed Life

- Love
- Joy
- Peace
- Patience
- Kindness
- Faithfulness
- Goodness

- Life is Christ-centered
- Empowered by Holy Spirit
- Introduces others to Christ
- Has effective prayer life
- Understands God's Word
- Trusts God
- Obeys God

- *(He draws continually upon the unlimited resources of God's love and power.)*

- *(He is alive to God because the Son of God is living in and through him.)*

- *(He brings glory to God because of his fruitful life and witness.)*

The *worldly person* is a believer trying to live the Christian life in his own strength (1 Corinthians 3:1–3).

Self-Directed Life

- Legalistic attitude
- Impure thoughts
- Jealousy
- Guilt
- Worry
- Discouragement
- Critical spirit
- Frustration
- Aimlessness
- Fear

- Ignorance of his spiritual heritage
- Unbelief
- Disobedience
- Loss of love for God and for others
- Poor prayer life
- No desire for Bible study

- *(He is a defeated and fruitless Christian.)*

- *(He depends on his own abilities rather than on the Holy Spirit.)*

- *(He lives in frustration and slavery to sin.)*

Read Romans 7:14–20, then give the following illustration: Unconfessed sin short-circuits the flow of God's power in your life. Let me illustrate. One day, as Bill Bright was operating the controls of his son's electric train, it suddenly stopped running. He could not figure out what was wrong. He took the train apart and put it back together. He pushed the plug in and out of the socket; nothing happened. Then he discovered that a small piece of metal—a No Left Turn sign—had fallen across the positive and negative rails, short-circuiting all the electric power.

To maintain a victorious Christian life and live as a spiritual Christian, you must keep short accounts with God. This means that you must keep God's power active in your life by confessing (agree that your sin is wrong and change your attitude and actions) any sin that enters your life the moment God's Holy Spirit reveals it to you. If you refuse to confess your sin, you will short-circuit your communication with God and will become worldly and walk in the shadow instead of in the light of God's love and forgiveness.

Ask the group to complete the sentence following diagram 3 in their books.

Read Romans 7:25–8:11. Explain: The worldly Christian can cease being worldly and experience God's love and forgiveness by faith.

Ask and discuss: If Christ has already paid the penalty for our sins, why should we confess them? *(By confessing sin, we act on our faith in God and His Word. Confession doesn't give us more forgiveness. Christ has already forgiven us once and for all. But by admitting our sins, we establish in our experience what God has done for us through the death of His Son.)*

Does God stop loving us when we sin? *(No. God loves us not "when," "if," or "because" we deserve it, but even when we are disobedient and rebellious. But if we refuse to deal honestly with God by ignoring our sins, we interfere with God's work in our lives. Further, as a disobedient child is disciplined by a loving parent, so God disciplines us when we live lives of disobedience.)*

Read Psalm 32:1–5, then answer the questions.

1. What was King David's experience when he refused to confess his sins? *(He was miserable; his strength was drained; he experienced guilt feelings.)*

2. What happened when he acknowledged his sin? *(He experienced a release from guilt and received joy in his life.)*

Spiritual Breathing

Read Hebrews 11:1,6. Ask: How does Hebrews 11:1 describe faith? *(Assurance of things hoped for, conviction of things not seen.)* How would you apply that verse in your life on a day-to-day basis? **Allow for varied responses. Explain:** By faith through an act of our will, we can experience Christ's resurrection power and life as we are filled with the Holy Spirit.

Say: The worldly person can appropriate God's solution for sin and become a spiritual Christian by practicing Spiritual Breathing. **Describe the process of physical breathing.** When you breathe, you exhale impurities like carbon dioxide and inhale the pure like oxygen. Spiritual Breathing is *exhaling* the impure (confessing our sins) and *inhaling* the pure (appropriating the power of God's Spirit as an act of our will by faith). We "exhale spiritually" when we confess our sins according to God's promise in 1 John 1:9, repent (or change our attitude toward our sins), and change our behavior through the power of the Holy Spirit.

Compare what happens to your body if you stop breathing with what happens to your spiritual life if you do not confess your sins. Emphasize that you cannot lose your spiritual life but you can become useless to God because you are bound by sin.

Handling Guilt

Ask: Where does guilt come from? *(Guilty feelings come from two sources. God's Holy Spirit may be convicting you of sin or Satan may be trying to defeat you by reminding you of old sins that you have confessed.)*

Explain the difference between real guilt and false guilt. *(The Holy Spirit convicts us of specific sins. Once you have sincerely repented and confessed your sin to God, any guilt feelings concerning it thereafter are false. You may, however, still suffer consequences of your sin, but the guilt has been lifted. False guilt, on the other hand, is a vague sense of sinfulness. It arises when there is no reason to feel guilty.)*

Ask: How can I tell if my guilt is real or false? **Discuss the checklist for handling guilt in the Study Guide. Encourage the students to use the checklist in the future whenever they feel guilty.**

Application (5–8 minutes)

Using the Action Point in the Student Lesson Plan, lead your students in *exhaling* spiritually—confessing their sins. Give your group a few minutes to follow the steps for exhaling. Then, without asking group members to reveal personal situations or commitments, discuss ways Chris-

tians can make restitution if they have wronged someone. Give an example of restitution to clarify the concept.

Closing and Prayer (2–3 minutes)

Challenge your students to keep short accounts with God this week and to note the results in their daily lives.

Close with a brief prayer; mention each member of your group by name. Thank God for the fact that He will fulfill His promise of abundant life and that He will restore our fellowship with Him whenever we sincerely repent and confess our sins. Explain that next week we will learn how to *inhale* spiritually—to be filled with the Spirit.

Follow-up

Update your 3×5 cards with any new praises or needs in your group. Keep praying daily for your students.

Student Lesson Plan

The Problem of Sin

1. Who has sinned? (Romans 3:23)

2. How did the sin of Adam, the father of the human race, affect you? (Romans 5:12)

3. What is the difference between temptation and sin?

   - Who is the tempter? (Matthew 4:1)

   - What causes you to be drawn into temptation? (James 1:13–15)

   - How does sin differ from temptation?

What Is the Basis for Our Forgiveness?

1. According to John 1:29, what is Jesus called and what does He do?

Read Hebrews 10:1–18.

2. What did Jesus do for our sins?

   Was this acceptable to God?

3. What did the sacrifice of Jesus accomplish for us?

4. How many of your sins did Christ forgive?

The Power of Sin

According to Romans 6:1–18, Christ not only died for our sin and forgave it, He also delivered us from sin's power.

1. What does God's Word tell you happened to your old sin nature when you became a Christian?

2. According to verse 11, what must you do?

3. According to verses 16 and 17, what choice faces you continuously?

4. What limit does God place on the temptations you face? (1 Corinthians 10:13)

5. What does God promise to provide you with when you are tempted?

Three Types of People

The Bible describes three types of people in 1 Corinthians, chapters 2 and 3. Underline the characteristics of each. Determine which type of life you are living.

- The *natural person* (1 Corinthians 2:14) is not a Christian. He depends on his own resources and lives in his own strength. Spiritually, he is dead to God—separated from God by sin.

Self-Directed Life

S – Self is on the throne

† – Christ is outside the life

● – Interests are directed by self, often resulting in discord and frustration

- The *spiritual person* (1 Corinthians 2:15,16) is a Christian who is controlled and empowered by the Holy Spirit. He draws upon the unlimited resources of God's love and power and lives in the strength of the living Christ. He is alive to God because the Son of God is living in and through him. He brings glory to God because of his fruitful life and witness.

Christ-Directed Life

- Love
- Joy
- Peace
- Patience
- Kindness
- Faithfulness
- Goodness

- Life is Christ-centered
- Empowered by Holy Spirit
- Introduces others to Christ
- Has effective prayer life
- Understands God's Word
- Trusts God
- Obeys God

■ The *worldly person* (1 Corinthians 3:1–3) is a believer trying to live the Christian life in his own strength. He is a defeated, fruitless Christian, who depends on his own abilities instead of drawing upon the inexhaustible resources of the Holy Spirit. He lives in frustration and slavery to sin (Romans 7:14–20).

Self-Directed Life
- Legalistic attitude
- Impure thoughts
- Jealousy
- Guilt
- Worry
- Discouragement
- Critical spirit
- Frustration
- Aimlessness
- Fear

- Ignorance of his spiritual heritage
- Unbelief
- Disobedience
- Loss of love for God and for others
- Poor prayer life
- No desire for Bible study

I am living the life of the _____ person.

Read Psalm 32:1–5.

1. What was King David's experience when he refused to confess his sins?

2. What happened when he acknowledged his sin?

Spiritual Breathing

A spiritual man lives by faith in God. Faith is trusting that God will do what He says He will do. When we place our faith in God and His Word, we can experience His love and power.

How can we get off the emotional, roller-coaster existence of a worldly life? By practicing "Spiritual Breathing," which is *exhaling* the impure (confessing our sins) and *inhaling* the pure (appropriating the power of the Holy Spirit as an act of our will by faith), 1 John 1:9; Ephesians 5:18.

Handling Guilt

When you feel guilty, compare your feelings to the criteria in this checklist, then circle the correct responses below. Follow the directions you have circled.

Checklist for Finding the Source of Guilt
When the Holy Spirit convicts me of sin:
■ He will point out a specific sin, and
■ God will forgive the sin and restore my fellowship with Him as soon as I confess it. The guilt is immediately lifted.
I am feeling false guilt if:
■ My feelings of guilt are vague and unspecific, or
■ I feel guilty over a sin that I previously and sincerely confessed to God.
Circle one: My feelings of guilt are (real) (false) so I will (exhale—confess it to God) (thank God that His forgiveness is immediate and complete).

Action Point: To *exhale,* follow these steps:

1. Ask the Lord to reveal any unconfessed sins. Write them on a piece of paper.

2. Confess these sins (agree with God that they are wrong).

3. Write 1 John 1:9 across the top. Destroy the list.

4. Make plans for restitution where you have wronged someone.

How You Can Be Filled With the Holy Spirit

Focus

Being filled with the Holy Spirit by faith is an act of our will.

Objectives

This session will help students to:

- *Identify* the Person and ministry of the Holy Spirit and what it means to be filled with the Spirit
- *Understand* how to be filled with the Spirit
- *Make a decision* to be filled with the Spirit

Session Scriptures

John 15:1–5,8; Galatians 5:22,23; Matthew 4:19; Ephesians 5:18–20; 1 John 5:14,15

Resources to Help You Lead the Study

- Transferable Concept: *How You Can Be Filled With the Spirit*
- *Ten Basic Steps Toward Christian Maturity: The Christian and the Holy Spirit*
- *The Holy Spirit: The Key to Supernatural Living*

Outline

I. Who is the Holy Spirit?
II. Why did the Holy Spirit come?

III. What does is mean to be filled with the Spirit?
IV. The fruits of the Spirit
V. How to be filled with the Holy Spirit

Leader's Preparation

The following comments may help you if questions arise about the verses to be studied in this lesson.

John 15:1–5,8. This passage about the vine and the branches clearly reinforces the truth that God is the only source of spiritual life; no branch can produce fruit on its own.

Galatians 5:22,23. The fruit of the Spirit is singular, not a miscellaneous collection of individual personal qualities. When the Spirit is at work in a life, all the qualities will be growing, even though a person may be giving primary attention to one particular area at a time.

Matthew 4:19. Following Jesus involves much more than mere assent to His teachings. He calls us to follow His example of reaching out to others.

Ephesians 5:18–20. Being filled with God's Spirit is a continuing action. This is not a one-time moment of submission, but a lifestyle of surrendering control of every area of your life to Christ.

1 John 5:14,15. It is definitely God's will that we be filled with His Spirit. When you ask Him to control and direct your life, you can be sure He will answer your prayer.

The Transferable Concept: *How You Can Be Filled With the Holy Spirit* expands the message in this lesson. Read it thoroughly to help you lead the study. Bring a flip chart or large sheet of paper to write on.

The Bible Study Session

Remember these directions for using this lesson:

- **The leader's directions are in bold type.**

- **The answers to questions are in parentheses and italicized.**

- **Have members fill out their books during the study.**

Sharing (Up to 5 minutes)

Invite students to share their progress in Spiritual Breathing. Ask: How difficult has it been to confess your sin as soon as you were aware of it? What effect has confessing your sin had on your relationship with Christ this past week? **Affirm each person's response, avoiding the temptation to tell them to do better. Emphasize that beginning a new behavior is sometimes difficult.**

Discussion Starter (8–10 minutes)

Say: Last week we observed three circles representing three types of lives. **Review the diagrams from the Study Guide in Lesson 2.**

Say: We also discussed the first step of Spiritual Breathing— *exhaling* or confession of sins. **Review the steps for *exhaling* from the last lesson.**

Say: This week, we will concentrate on the second step— *inhaling* or appropriating the fullness of the Holy Spirit by faith. **Review the similarities between physical breathing and Spiritual Breathing.**

Lesson Development (30–40 minutes)

Explain: The Christian life is a great adventure. It is a life of purpose and power. Indeed, Christ gives us the almost unbelievable promise, "I tell you the truth, anyone who has faith in me will do what I have been doing. He will do even greater things than these, because I am going to the Father. And I will do whatever you ask in my name, so that the Son may bring glory to the Father" (John 14:12,13).

Obviously, we cannot accomplish these great works in our own energy. It is Christ Himself—living within us, in all His resurrection power, walking around in our bodies, thinking with our minds, loving with our hearts, speaking with our lips—who will empower us with the Holy Spirit to do these great works.

Yet, many Christians do not know who the Holy Spirit is or how to appropriate His power. Consequently, they go through life without experiencing the abundant and fruitful life Christ promised to all who trust Him.

Before we can understand the filling of the Holy Spirit, we need to know more about the person of the Holy Spirit.

Who Is the Holy Spirit?

Look up the following verses and discuss the questions. Have the students write their answers in their books.

- Acts 5:3,4 *(He is God.)*

- 1 Thessalonians 5:19; Ephesians 4:30 *(He is a person with feelings.)*

  How do you know He is a person and not a force or impersonal power? 1 Corinthians 2:11 *(He has thoughts.)*; 1 Corinthians 12:11 *(He has a will.)*; Romans 15:30 *(He loves.)*

- Matthew 28:19; 2 Corinthians 13:14 *(He is the third person of the Trinity.)*

- What did Jesus call the Holy Spirit in John 14:16,17? *(Helper, Comforter.)*

Holy Spirit

Draw the diagram on the flip chart, then explain: The Holy Spirit is the third person of the Trinity: Father, Son, and Holy Spirit. Each person of the Trinity is equal in every way and is not separate from one another. Just as an apple has a core, flesh, and peel, so the Trinity exists in three distinct personalities that are separate yet are completely one. Each person of the Trinity performs different functions. **You may find that some students are confused about the Holy Spirit's role in the Trinity or others may want to introduce controversial ideas throughout this lesson. Don't get into issues not covered in the lesson material. Instead, refer students to the book *The Holy Spirit: The Key to Supernatural Living*. For order information, see the Resources section in the back of this Guide.**

Why Did the Holy Spirit Come?

Look up the verses and answer this question together.

- John 3:5 *(To bring us into the kingdom of God.)*

- John 16:7,8,13,14 *(To lead us into all truth, to convict us of sin, to tell us of things to come, to glorify Christ.)*

- John 7:37–39 *(Receiving living water means to give us joyful, abundant life.)*

- Acts 1:8 *(To help us witness.)*

- Romans 8:26 *(To help us pray.)*

- Ephesians 1:13,14 *(To guarantee our spiritual inheritance as children of God.)*

What Does It Mean to Be Filled With the Spirit?

Read: There is only one indwelling of the Holy Spirit, one rebirth of the Holy Spirit, and one baptism of the Holy Spirit. They occur when you receive Christ.

Being filled with the Spirit, however, is not a once-for-all experience. There are many fillings, as is made clear in Ephesians

5:18. **Read the verse, then point out the following explana-
tion, which is also in the Student Lesson Plan.** *(To be filled
with the Spirit is to be filled with Jesus Christ, the risen Son of God,
and to abide in Him. Since God is one shown through three persons,
the Holy Spirit is the essence of Jesus. Filled means to be directed,
controlled, and empowered by the Holy Spirit.)*

Explain: In the Greek language in which the command to "be
filled with the Spirit" was originally written, the meaning is clearer
than in most English translations. This command of God means
to be constantly and continually filled, controlled, and empowered
with the Holy Spirit as a way of life.

Ask: What is the difference between being filled with wine and
being filled with the Spirit? **Focus on the negative effect of
being filled with wine versus the positive result of being
filled with the Spirit.**

Ask: Why is a person different when he is filled with either
one of these agents? *(Because each controls the individual and
produces a change in behavior.)*

Say: Think of it! Can you grasp what this means? If you yield
your will to God the Holy Spirit and let Him control you moment
by moment, your life will become a great adventure.

The Fruits of the Spirit

**Ask half your group to read John 15:1–5 and answer
question 1 in the Study Guide; have the rest read verse 8
and answer question 2 in the Study Guide. Allow two or
three minutes for students to read their verse(s). Ask volunteers to share answers:**

1. What comparisons can you draw between the relationship
   of the vine to a branch and of Christ to a Christian? *(Just as
   a branch lives and produces fruit by being linked to the vine,
   so a Christian lives and produces fruit by being linked to the
   life and power of Christ through the Holy Spirit.)*

2. What does "fruit" mean in verse 8? *(The characteristics produced by the Holy Spirit in a Christian's life.)*

Read Matthew 4:19, Galatians 5:22, and Ephesians 5:18–20 aloud one at a time. Ask a volunteer to list the characteristics of the Spirit-filled life on the flip chart. Discuss which qualities are the hardest for the group members to apply personally.

Ask: Which fruits have you been trusting God to develop within you? **Allow individuals to respond.**

Ask: God works to develop His fruit in the life of a person who is filled with the Holy Spirit. What are some specific changes you hope to see as God produces His fruit in you? **Give an example from your life first, then invite your group to respond individually also. Do not press students to reveal personal decisions.**

Explain: A new Christian should not become discouraged if he does not bear as much fruit as a more mature Christian who has been abiding in Christ for some time. The new Christian can be just as spiritual as the more mature Christian because the same life of the Vine is in both. He can look forward to maturing and producing more fruit as he continually draws on the life of the Vine over a period of time.

How to Be Filled With the Holy Spirit

Say: Learning how to be filled with the Holy Spirit is the most important discovery of the Christian life. **Point out "How to Be Filled With the Holy Spirit" in the Student Lesson Plan. Discuss why many Christians are not living Spirit-filled lives.** *(Because of a lack of knowledge or because of unbelief.)*

Ask: What is keeping you from being filled with the Holy Spirit? **Give students time to write their answers in their books.**

Ask: Does an emotional experience or dramatic event always accompany being filled with the Spirit? **Compare receiving**

Christ by faith with being filled with the Spirit by faith. Bring out these points: Do not think that you have to have an emotional experience or that something dramatic must happen to you. How did you receive Christ? Was it because of some great emotional pressure brought to bear upon you? Your emotions may have been involved. But ultimately you became a Christian, not because of an emotional experience, but because of your faith as an act of your will.

The Holy Spirit is not given to you that you might have a great emotional experience, but that you might live a holy life and be a fruitful witness for Christ.

Say: Read the definition for *inhaling* spiritually in your Study Guide. There are two important words to remember: "command" and "promise." The command is found in Ephesians 5:18. We are commanded to be filled with the Spirit. The promise is given in 1 John 5:14,15 and makes the command possible. **Read the verse aloud.**

Discuss: How do you know it is God's will for you to be filled with the Holy Spirit? *(He commanded it as recorded in Ephesians 5:18.)* When can you ask God to fill you with His Spirit? *(Right now, not because I deserve to be filled, but on the basis of God's grace and His promise in 1 John 5:14,15.)*

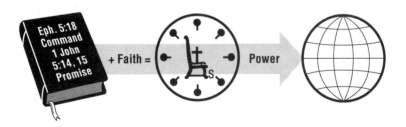

Application (5 minutes)

Encourage your students to apply the Action Point of Spiritual Breathing. The steps below are given in the Study Guide also.

Exhale:

- Ask the Holy Spirit to show you any unconfessed sin.
- Confess your sin and claim the promise of 1 John 1:9.
- Make restitution if necessary.

Inhale:

- Claim the filling of the Holy Spirit by faith on the basis of God's *command* and God's *promise* (Ephesians 5:18, 1 John 5:14,15).

After giving your students time to do Spiritual Breathing, ask the following questions. Be sensitive to individual needs of group members.

1. Did you ask God to fill you with the Holy Spirit? **Allow time for individual responses.**

2. Do you know that you are now filled with the Holy Spirit? **Let students answer.**

3. On what authority? *(The promise of God's Word.)*

Closing and Prayer (2–5 minutes)

Say: Everyone please bow your heads in an attitude of prayer. If the prayer I am about to offer expresses your desire for God to fill you with His Holy Spirit, please pray silently with me. The prayer is printed in your Study Guide.

Lead your students in the prayer at the end of the Student Lesson Plan. Encourage them to practice Spiritual Breathing during the week. Before dismissing the group, inform them that next week the lesson will be on learning how to walk in the Spirit for a fruitful, abundant life.

Follow-up

During the week, practice Spiritual Breathing. Take note of the results. Come prepared to share your experiences with your group.

Student Lesson Plan

Answer the following questions from the verses given.

Who Is the Holy Spirit?

- Acts 5:3,4

- 1 Thessalonians 5:19; Ephesians 4:30

  How do you know He is a person and not a force or impersonal power? 1 Corinthians 2:11; 12:11; Romans 15:30

- Matthew 28:19; 2 Corinthians 13:14

- What did Jesus call the Holy Spirit in John 14:16,17?

Why Did the Holy Spirit Come?

- John 3:5

- John 16:7,8,13,14

- John 7:37–39

- Acts 1:8

- Romans 8:26

- Ephesians 1:13,14

What Does It Mean to Be Filled With the Spirit?

To be filled with the Spirit is to be filled with Jesus Christ, the risen Son of God, and to abide in Him. Since God is one shown through three persons, the Holy Spirit is the essence of Jesus.

Filled means to be directed, controlled, and empowered by the Holy Spirit. When I am filled with the Spirit, Christ's Spirit will dwell in my body and live His resurrection life in and through me.

1. What is the difference between being filled with wine and being filled with the Spirit?

2. Why is a person different when he is filled with either one of these agents?

The Fruits of the Spirit

Read John 15:1–5,8.

1. What comparison can you draw between the relationship of a vine to a branch and of Christ to a Christian?

2. What does "fruit" mean in verse 8?

How to Be Filled With the Holy Spirit

Although all Christians are indwelt by the Spirit, not all are filled with the Spirit. Most Christians are not filled with the Spirit because of:

- Lack of knowledge
- Unbelief

What is keeping you from being filled with the Spirit?

Action Point: To be filled with the Spirit, practice Spiritual Breathing.

Exhale:

- Ask the Holy Spirit to show you any unconfessed sin.

- Confess your sin and claim the promise of 1 John 1:9.

- Make restitution if necessary.

Inhale:

- Claim the filling of the Holy Spirit by faith on the basis of God's *command* and God's *promise* (Ephesians 5:18, 1 John 5:14,15).

Here is a prayer you can use:

Dear Father, I need You. I acknowledge that I have been in control of my own life and have sinned against You. I thank You for forgiving my sins through Christ's death on the cross for me. I now invite Christ to take control of my life. Fill me with the Holy Spirit as You commanded me to be filled. You promised in Your Word that You would fill me if I ask in faith. As an expression of my faith, I now thank You for filling me with Your Holy Spirit and for taking control of my life. Amen.

How You Can Walk In the Spirit

Focus

Walking in the Spirit is a moment-by-moment experience.

Objectives

This session will help students to:

- *Define* "how to walk in the Spirit"

- *Identify* three barriers that keep a Christian from walking in the Spirit and *understand* how to deal with those barriers

- *Practice* Spiritual Breathing throughout the week

Session Scriptures

Romans 7:15–20; Ephesians 5:18; 1 John 1:9

Resources to Help You Lead the Study

- Transferable Concept: *How You Can Walk in the Spirit*

Outline

    I. The Christian life
   II. Spiritual conflict
  III. Barriers to walking in the Spirit
      A. Barrier of unconfessed sin
      B. Barrier of self effort
      C. Barrier of circumstances
  IV. Dealing with barriers

Leader's Preparation

God not only desires for us to have a relationship with Him, but He also wants our fellowship as well (1 Corinthians 1:9; 1 John 1:3). The difference between relationship and fellowship can be illustrated by the father/son connection in a human family. When a baby boy is born, he is the son of his father because he has his father's life in him. He bears his father's name. If the son rebels and leaves home, is he still the son of the father? Of course.

The relationship of a father and son is permanent. The son, however, may not always enjoy the fellowship of the father. Comradeship can be damaged if not completely destroyed. In such a case, what must the son do to restore the fellowship? He must go to his father, admit his wrongs, and ask for forgiveness.

Our relationship with our Father, God, is permanent (John 10:27–29). We have His life within us, and we bear the name of Christ. What happens, then, when we sin? Is our relationship ended? Is His life removed from us? Of course not.

Fellowship between Christians and God, however, can be damaged and broken. To have this fellowship restored, we must tell God we have been wrong and ask Him for forgiveness.

The Transferable Concept: *How You Can Walk in the Spirit* expands the message in this lesson. Read it thoroughly to help you lead the study. Bring a flip chart or large sheet of paper to write on. Also bring a Bible that has a good concordance in the back. Learn how to use it so you can teach your group how to use it.

The Bible Study Session

Remember these directions for using this lesson:

- **The leader's directions are in bold type.**
- **The answers to questions are in parentheses and italicized.**
- **Have members fill out their books during the study.**

Sharing (5–10 minutes)

Say: Turn to the graph "My Christian Walk" in your Study Guide. As best you can, chart your spiritual well-being for the past few weeks, showing any "highs" or "lows" or steady progress you have made in applying Spiritual Breathing. **Example:**

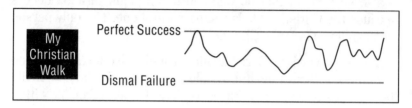

Share your experiences of Spiritual Breathing from the last week. Ask your students to pair up and share their graph with a partner.

Discussion Starter (5 minutes)

Discuss these four statements:

1. If I walk in the Spirit, I will be free from difficulties. *(No. Problems of poor health, loss of loved ones, financial needs, and other such experiences are common to all people.)*

2. A spiritually mature person can still sin. *(Yes. All people, no matter how spiritually mature in Christ, experience temptation and have tendencies to sin.)*

3. A mature Christian is more "spiritual" than a less mature Christian. *(No. Each of us has access to the full power of the Holy Spirit. We are all at different spiritual growth stages, but we can all be directed by the Holy Spirit moment by moment.)*

4. A person must be a Christian many years to walk daily with the Lord. *(No. The moment a person receives Christ as Savior, he can walk in the Spirit. Walking in the Spirit—consciously trusting the Holy Spirit to guide and empower all areas of living—is possible for a new believer as well as for one who is mature. Maturity, however, will increase sensitivity to the Spirit's leading.)*

Lesson Development (30–40 minutes)

The Christian Life

Read: The Christian life is not complex or difficult. It is so simple that we sometimes stumble over the simplicity of it. Yet it is also so difficult that no one can live it! This paradox occurs because the Christian life is a supernatural one. The only person who can live it is Jesus Christ.

If we try to live the Christian life through self effort, we will find it complex, difficult, and impossible to accomplish. But if we invite the Lord Jesus to direct our lives, He lives His abundant life within us in all His resurrection power.

Walking in the Spirit, then, is living according to God's promise, trusting in the integrity of God Himself. Faith must have an object, and the object of your faith is God, made known through His Word. When God says something, you can stake your life on it. He will not fail you.

Discuss: What does John 14:21 say about a life of trusting God? *(We obey Him because we love Him. As we love and obey Him, we experience His love, and He reveals Himself to us.)*

Spiritual Conflict

Explain: The Bible explains that there are three forces—the world, the flesh (human nature with its desires and weaknesses), and the devil—that constantly wage war against the believer. Let us look briefly at each of these forces.

1. The World

Read 1 John 2:15–17. What are some things that the world offers? **On the flip chart, make a list of worldly things from the verses.**

Discuss: What are some ways in which the world affects us? *(The lure of materialism, success, or fame.)* How can we resist the influence of the world? *(Stop loving the world. Remember that these things will pass away. Do the will of God.)*

Barriers to Walking in the Spirit

1. Barrier of Unconfessed Sin

Say: A Christian must be alert to things in life that can damage the quality of his walk in the Spirit. **Discuss the difference between fellowship and relationship. Present the illustration of the father/son relationship from the Leader's Preparation. Work together through the section "Barrier of Unconfessed Sin" in the Student Lesson Plan.** *(Answers to chart: A–2,5,6; B–1,3,4,6.)*

Say: Practicing Spiritual Breathing is a means to deal with unconfessed sin. **Have the students pair up and list the steps of Spiritual Breathing in their books. The steps are listed in Lesson 3.**

2. Barrier of Self-Effort

Read Romans 7:15–20. Work together to answer the questions in the Student Lesson Plan:

1. What is the source of Paul's struggle in this passage? *(Paul clearly saw self-effort as inadequate to cope with the challenges of sin against his desire to do good.)*

2. How did that make him feel? *(Paul felt frustrated and discouraged.)*

3. Have you experienced similar frustration? *(You may have varied responses. New Christians may not have encountered deep struggles with temptation; others hesitate to tell the group of personal defeats.)* **Share a personal example to help the group share their experiences.**

Assure the group that it is not necessary for anyone to share the details of an experience, but it is helpful to know that struggles in this area of self-effort are not unique.

Discuss: Where do works fit in? *(Many Christians think of "spiritual" good works—Bible study, prayer, or any other spiritual discipline—as the means to, rather than the results of, a life of faith.*

They spend much energy on works, hoping they will achieve the abundant Christian life. They put their faith and much effort into "doing" things to please God, rather than in appropriating God's power to live the Christian life by faith. But they remain defeated and discouraged. So they spend more time on self-effort, which leads to greater defeat and frustration. Good works are the visible evidence that we are being filled and controlled by the Holy Spirit, not the way we become Spirit-filled.)

Discuss: How can we keep from relying on self-effort? *(Be thankful, 1 Thessalonians 5:18; Rest in the Lord, Psalm 37:7; Learn from Jesus, Matthew 11:29,30; Keep your eyes on God, Isaiah 40:21–26.)* **Encourage students to give specific examples of how they plan to do this.**

3. Barrier of Circumstances

Refer the students to the section "Barrier of Circumstances" in their Study Guides. Explain: Remember the train diagram from Lesson 1? When fuel is available to the engine, the train runs. Trying to pull the train by the caboose would be foolish. In a similar way, we should not depend on feelings to live the Christian life. We should place our trust in God and His Word. Feelings are like the caboose. They will follow when we put our faith in God, but they should never pull the train.

When we trust God with our circumstances, He will guide us through them and give us victory over them. How does Romans 8:28 give you confidence in difficult circumstances? *(God has promised to work all things for good if we love Him and obey Him.)* Think of a situation that looked hopeless yet God turned to good. **Allow students to respond.**

Ask: How can we learn how to walk in the Spirit if we have weak faith? *(Faith must have an object. We do not have faith in faith itself.)*

Say: We can strengthen our faith. For example, an ice fisherman has faith that the ice on a lake is thick enough to support his weight. Because of this faith, he boldly walks out on thin ice and gets very wet. On the other hand, another ice fisherman with weak faith moves slowly onto thick ice. As he inches out, he realizes its ability to support his weight and his faith grows. Soon he brings his ice house onto the ice and begins fishing.

So it is in the Christian life. We place our faith, even one that is weak, in a trustworthy object: God and His Word. The better we know God, the more we can trust Him. The more we trust Him, the more we experience the reality of His love and grace and power. Faith is like muscle—it grows with exercise.

Ask the students to describe situations that have strengthened their faith.

Ask: How can you be sure you are walking by faith rather than feelings? *(One way is to memorize Scripture verses that emphasize God's promise or will in a certain area and recall the verses to check your feelings by the Word of God. Another is to use a Bible concordance.)* **Explain how a good Bible concordance can help you find verses that deal with many subjects. Show your group the concordance in the back of their Bibles. Look up what God has to say about a particular topic such as worry or fear, and discuss how using the verses you find can help you avoid letting feelings control your reaction. Also show your students how to use cross-references.**

Dealing With Barriers

Discuss these questions:

- What are some facts we can trust about God and our relationship with Him? **Read Romans 8:38,39.** *(Nothing can separate us from God and His love.)*

- What happens when we place our faith in these facts? *(God gives us power to deal with sin, 1 Corinthians 10:13; circumstances, Romans 8:30,31; and tendencies toward self-effort, Matthew 11:28,29. We experience joy and peace, John 15:11; Philippians 4:7.)*

■ How would your life be affected by putting trust in your feelings instead of in God's Word? *(We would become frustrated and confused.)*

Ask the students to list in their Study Guides three difficult areas in their lives, such as dating, finances, or family concerns. Give the students a few minutes to do this, then discuss how placing faith in God's Word would affect each circumstance.

Say: Giving thanks is a practical way to demonstrate faith.

Go through the questions in the Study Guide.

1. What does God promise in Romans 8:28? *(He will work all things together for our good.)*

2. What are we commanded to do in 1 Thessalonians 5:18? *(To give thanks at all times.)*

3. Have you ever tried this in difficult circumstances? What happened? **Allow for individual responses.**

4. What is a result of being filled with the Holy Spirit according to Ephesians 5:20? *(Giving thanks for all things.)*

Help your students express their difficulties with giving thanks in difficult situations. Explain that walking in the Spirit is a process of maturing. The more you practice this as a way of life, the more you will do it when trials come.

Explain: Giving thanks under all circumstances demonstrates your faith in God. By giving thanks, you are saying, "God, I trust You." **Emphasize that the Bible does not tell us that we must *feel* thankful, but just to give thanks as an act of the will. Our feelings will follow as we obey.**

Explain: The following chart illustrates the difference between a life of self effort and a life of walking in the Spirit. **Go over the Action Point and the chart to help them practice faith and obedience during the next week.**

Walking in the Spirit	Trusts in God and His Word	Experiences forgiveness through confession	Believes God in order to be filled with His Spirit	God causes growth and fruitfulness
Walking in Self-Effort	Trusts in self	Sin brings guilt or rationalization	Increased effort to live by God's standards	Frustration and defeat

Application (3–5 minutes)

Ask students to share how they could put into practice their desire to grow in an area they listed in the Action Point. You could suggest:

- *(Setting a regular time for prayer and Bible study)*

- *(Memorizing Bible verses that deal with the area)*

- *(Practicing Spiritual Breathing)*

- *(Remembering God's past work in their life during stressful times)*

Closing and Prayer (3–5 minutes)

Thank God for His Spirit's presence and support in meeting the difficulties we face. Explain: Next week will be our last session. We will be learning how to plan intimate time with God each day. I appreciate the openness and faithfulness you all have given to this group. I have learned so much through your contributions to the Bible study.

Follow-up

Update your cards on needs for which your students have requested prayer. Some group members may appreciate personal visits to pray over their problems or just to enjoy fellowship. Or plan a social gathering, such as a picnic or potluck dinner. This will help you see your students in a different atmosphere.

Student Lesson Plan

As best you can, chart your spiritual well-being for the past few weeks, showing any "highs" or "lows" or steady progress you have made in applying Spiritual Breathing.

```
┌─────────────────────────────────────────────────────────┐
│  ████████                                                 │
│  █ My █    Perfect Success ─────────────────────────────  │
│ Christian                                                 │
│  █Walk█                                                   │
│  ████████   Dismal Failure ─────────────────────────────  │
└─────────────────────────────────────────────────────────┘
```

Spiritual Conflict

Read Romans 7:14–25.

1. What was Paul's opinion of his flesh?

2. When we received Christ, in what new position were we placed in relation to Christ? (Ephesians 2:6)

3. What happened to us because of our position in Christ? (Romans 6:5,6)

4. What happened to our old sin nature?

5. What must we do to have victory over the flesh?

   ▪ Romans 6:11

   ▪ Galatians 5:16,17

Barriers to Walking in the Spirit

1. Barrier of Unconfessed Sin

Sin will not affect our relationship with God; that is permanent. Sin, however, will break our fellowship with God. Match the statements on the left with the answers on the right.

A. Our relationship with God is:	1. Restored by confessing sin
	2. Maintained by God
	3. Capable of being broken
	4. Maintained in part by us
B. Our fellowship with God is:	5. Eternally secure
	6. Begun at salvation

Practicing Spiritual Breathing is a means to deal with unconfessed sin. List the steps to Spiritual Breathing (refer to Lesson 3).

1.

2.

3.

4.

2. Barrier of Self-Effort

Read Romans 7:15–20.

1. What is the source of Paul's struggle in this passage?

2. How did that make him feel?

3. When have you experienced similar frustration?

3. Barrier of Circumstances

Many Christians allow circumstances to sway their faith. But we are to live by faith and believe in the trustworthiness of God's Word. The train diagram illustrates the relationship between:

- Fact (God and His Word)

- Faith (our trust in God and His Word)

- Feeling (the result of our faith and obedience)

How can you be sure you are walking by faith rather than feelings?

Dealing With Barriers

List three areas of your life—such as dating, finances, or family concerns—and describe how placing your faith in God's Word would affect each circ umstance.

1.

2.

3.

Giving thanks is a practical way to demonstrate faith. Read the verses and answer the following questions.

1. What does God promise in Romans 8:28?

2. What are we commanded to do in 1 Thessalonians 5:18?

3. Have you ever tried this in difficult circumstances? What happened?

4. What is a result of being filled with the Holy Spirit according to Ephesians 5:20?

Action Point: Whenever a circumstance or temptation threatens to become a barrier between you and God this week, review this chart and reaffirm   your commitment to walk in the Spirit.

Walking in the Spirit	Trusts in God and His Word	Experiences for-giveness through confession	Believes God in order to be filled with His Spirit	God causes growth and fruitfulness
Walking in Self-Effort	Trusts in self	Sin brings guilt or rationalization	Increased effort to live by God's standards	Frustration and defeat

LESSON 5

How You Can Grow As a Christian

Focus

Growing in Christ involves reading the Bible, praying daily, having fellowship with other Christians, witnessing, and obeying God.

Objectives

This session will help students to:

- *Set up* a plan for a daily quiet time
- *Understand* the importance of fellowship to growing in Christ
- *List* people they will witness to the following week

Session Scriptures

Matthew 13:3–23; 2 Timothy 3:16; 1 Thessalonians 5:17; Hebrews 10:24,25; Romans 1:14–16; Luke 6:46–49

Resources to Help You Lead the Study

- Transferable Concepts:
  How You Can Pray With Confidence
  How You Can Be a Fruitful Witness
  How You Can Introduce Others to Christ

- *Ten Basic Steps Toward Christian Maturity: The Christian and Witnessing*

- *Life Without Equal*

Outline

    I. We must read the Bible.

    II. We must pray.

    III. We must fellowship with other Christians.

    IV. We must witness for Christ.

    V. We must obey God.

Leader's Preparation

Read the parable of the sower in Matthew 13:3–23. This illustration shows that some who hear the Word of God will not grow to spiritual maturity. But some who hear the Word will multiply themselves by introducing many others to Jesus Christ.

As you pray for each person in your group by referring to your 3×5 cards, ask the Lord to help you challenge each member to apply what they have learned. Praise God for the growth you have seen in their lives during the past few weeks. Write down a few notes on your vision for influencing your neighborhood and community for Christ. Bring the notes to the session.

Begin planning for another *Five Steps* Bible study as soon as this one ends. Some of your members may know of a friend, new believer, or family member who would like to be in this group. Ask your students to encourage others to come to the next study.

Bring a copy of the *Four Spiritual Laws* for each person in your group. See the Resources section at the back of this Guide for order information. Also bring a *Living Bible* and your flip chart.

The Bible Study Session

Remember these directions for using this lesson:

- **The leader's directions are in bold type.**

- **The answers to questions are in parentheses and italicized.**

- **Have members fill out their books during the study.**

Sharing (5 minutes)

Use this time to share your vision for influencing your neighborhood and community for Christ. Describe the problems you see and how God can help people rise above their circumstances. Tell of your love for those who don't know Christ and for Christians who are not walking close to God. Spend a few minutes in prayer for your local area. Ask God to help each group member see where God would have him influence his world for Christ.

Discussion Starter (5 minutes)

Read: Deciding to receive Jesus Christ as one's personal Lord and Savior is the most important decision of life. When you invited Christ into your life, you were born into God's family, and you received everything you need to live the abundant Christian life. That does not mean you are as spiritually mature as someone who has walked with Christ for many years. Just as physical life requires air, food, rest, and exercise, spiritual life requires certain things for growth and development.

Discuss: What happens to a child who doesn't grow properly in his physical body? In his emotional growth? In his spiritual maturity? How do these areas relate to each other?

Lesson Development (30–40 minutes)

Say: This lesson deals with five principles of growth. If these are followed, you will grow toward spiritual maturity in Christ. Let's go through each in your Study Guide.

Read 2 Peter 3:18. Ask: What is the result of spiritual growth? *(We become better acquainted with Jesus.)*

Principle One: We Must Read the Bible

Explain the diagram: The Christian who is allowing Christ to control his life is directed to read the Word of God, our spiritual food. Just as physical food is necessary for physical life, so spiritual food sustains spiritual life.

Allow the students a few minutes to look up the following verses and answer questions 1 through 3. Then discuss them as a group.

1. Jesus said, "Man shall not live by bread alone." How did He say that we should live and be nourished? Matthew 4:4 *(By every word that comes out of the mouth of God.)*

2. Why is reading God's Word so important? 2 Timothy 3:16, 17 *(The Bible teaches us how to live a life pleasing to God.)*

3. What will result in your life when you read God's Word? Psalm 119:11,105 *(I will be kept from sin and learn God's will for my life.)*

Ask if anyone in the group schedules time to read their Bible daily. Have those who say yes tell how daily Bible reading has enriched their lives.

Principle Two: We Must Pray

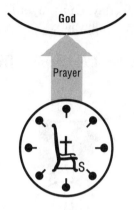

Explain the diagram: The Christ-controlled person is also instructed to pray or "talk to God." Look up the following verses and write your answers to the questions. **Allow five minutes of silence.**

Say: When praying, remember these things:

1. Pray about everything. Philippians 4:6,7.

   What is the result if we talk to God about everything? *(We won't worry, and we will have God's peace in our hearts.)*

2. Pray specifically. John 14:14, John 16:24.

   Why do you think it is important to pray specifically? *(To receive God's specific answers.)*

   What will be two results of praying specifically? *(We will receive specific answers, and our joy will be complete.)*

   Share a recent specific answer to prayer. Allow several students to share theirs.

3. Pray continually. 1 Thessalonians 5:17.

   What does the Bible mean when it says to pray continually? *(Talk to God about everything throughout the day.)*

Read John 14:13,14 aloud. Then say: Praying without ceasing involves talking to our heavenly Father in a simple and free way throughout the day. Our prayer life should help us know the Lord Jesus in a personal way.

Principle Three: We Must Fellowship With Other Christians

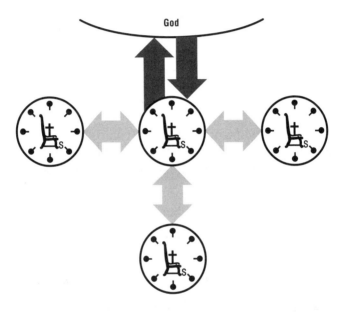

Explain the third diagram: As our lives are controlled by Christ, we will not only be directed to have fellowship with Him, but we will also reach out in fellowship to other Christians.

Read: Fellowship is spending time and doing things with others who love Christ. In a campfire, several logs burn brightly together, but place one alone on the cold ground and the fire goes out. In a similar way, Christians need to work together or the fire of enthusiasm will go out. Fellowship is vital for Christian growth. That is why church attendance is important.

Say: Let's take a few minutes to answer questions 1 through 5. **Give the students a few minutes to fill in their answers, then ask them to share what they wrote.**

1. As God's children, what should we not neglect? Hebrews 10:24,25. *(Gathering together in church.)* Why? *(For encouragement, training, and fellowship.)*

2. What are the basic functions of a local church? Colossians 1:25–27; 2 Timothy 4:2. *(To preach the Word of God; to build believers in their faith; to encourage and train Christians for more fruitful witness.)*

3. The new believers in the early church continued steadfastly in what four things? Acts 2:41,42.

   a. *(Baptism)*

   b. *(Teaching the Word of God)*

   c. *(The Lord's supper)*

   d. *(Prayer)*

4. If we spend 90 percent of our time with non-Christians and 10 percent with Christians, which group will have the greater influence on our lives? *(Non-Christians.)* Why? *(We are influenced by those around us. We learn habits, ways of thinking and acting from those closest to us.)*

Write on your flip chart: "Reasons for Joining a Church."

Let students give answers. Some responses include: *(To help meet the needs of other Christians. To receive encouragement and help during stressful times. To be trained to serve others.)*

Discuss what to look for in a church. Some answers are: *(A church that teaches from the Bible, that reaches out to unbelievers, where members care for each other.)*

Principle Four: We Must Witness for Christ

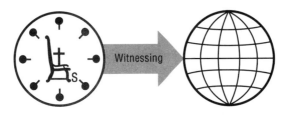

Explain the fourth diagram: As Christ controls our lives, we are also directed to tell non-Christians about Him.

One of the greatest acts of obedience is to share Christ with others in the power of the Holy Spirit. Since Jesus came to seek and save the lost (Luke 19:10) and has commissioned us to witness for Him (Matthew 28:18–20), nothing could please Him more. If you want a vital, exciting awareness of Christ in your daily life, faithfully witness for Christ as a way of life as you walk in the Spirit. Witnessing as a way of life is defined as simply taking the initiative to share Christ in the power of the Holy Spirit and leaving the results to God.

Read Colossians 1:28,29. Go through these questions from the Study Guide as a group:

1. What did Paul and the other believers do everywhere they went? *(They shared Christ—witnessed.)*

2. Why did they do this? *(That all might be perfect in Christ.)*

3. Where did they get the power to do this? *(From the Holy Spirit.)*

Say: Romans 3:21–25 tells us what our message should be to those who do not know God personally. **Read the verses from the *Living Bible*, then help students fill in the blanks in their books.**

1. In Romans 3:21, God says we cannot get to heaven by *(being good)* or by trying to keep His *(laws)*.

2. Romans 3:23,24 tell us that *(all)* have sinned and yet now God declares us not *(guilty)*, if we *(trust)* in Jesus Christ, who in His kindness freely takes away our *(sins)*.

3. Romans 3:25 says that God sent *(Jesus Christ)* to take the *(punishment)* for our sins and to end all God's anger against us. He used Christ's *(blood)* and our *(faith)* as the means of saving us from His wrath.

Pass out the *Four Spiritual Laws* booklets. Explain: The *Four Spiritual Laws* booklet is a clear and simple presentation of the good news God has for the world. The booklet can be used as an effective way to share your faith in Christ.

Here are some tips for using the *Four Spiritual Laws* booklets:

1. Share the claims of Christ as presented in the *Four Spiritual Laws* simply and clearly.

2. Without being pushy, invite people to pray to receive Christ. Leave the persuading to the Holy Spirit. However, be bold rather than uncertain in your presentation so your listeners will have confidence in what you are telling them.

3. If the person is not ready to receive Christ, be friendly and accepting so he will welcome the opportunity to talk about a personal relationship with Christ with either you or someone else at a later time.

Ask: What is a witness? *(A witness is a person who tells what he has seen and heard. He shares his own personal experience.)*

Who can witness for Christ? **Read Matthew 28:18–20.** *(Anyone who has a personal relationship with Christ can be a witness for Him.)*

Say: Let's take a few minutes to answer the next four questions and discover why we should witness. **Answer these questions as a group.**

1. What is the greatest thing that has ever happened to you? *(Coming to know Christ.)*

2. What, then, is the greatest thing that you can do for another person? *(Help someone come to know Christ.)*

3. In Romans 1:14-16, Paul tells us his own attitude about sharing the good news of Jesus Christ with others. Using his three "I's" as the keys to the passage, describe his attitude in your own words.

   (He felt obligated to share the good news of Jesus Christ with others.)
   (He was eager to share with others.)
   (He was not ashamed of sharing the gospel.)

4. What was Jesus' promise in Acts 1:8? *(We will receive power from the Holy Spirit to witness.)*

Discuss: Can you think of people with whom you could share the gospel? Perhaps it would be a neighbor, a relative, or a friend. **Encourage them to write the names down in their books.**

How will you witness to them? *(Simply share with them how you came to know Christ and explain the gospel by reading the Four Spiritual Laws booklet to them.)*

Principle Five: We Must Obey God

Read: The key to rapid growth in the Christian life is obedience to the will of God. Knowing the principles of growth is of no value unless we actually apply them to our lives. To be disobedient to the One who loves us and who alone knows what is really best for us would be sheer folly. Remember that He is even more desirous than you are that you have an abundant life.

Say: Look up the following verses and answer questions 1 through 4. **Allow the students to fill in their answers during a period of silence. Then ask them to read their answers.**

1. How can you prove that you love the Lord? John 14:21 *(By obeying His commandments.)*

2. What will be the result of keeping Christ's commandments? John 15:10 *(I will abide in Christ's love.)* What does that mean to you?

3. Where do we get the power to obey God? Philippians 2:13 *(From God.)*

4. In light of Christ's illustration in Luke 6:46–49, why would you say that obedience to Christ is imperative for your life? *(To maintain an unshakable fellowship with Christ.)*

Using the following diagram, discuss how the five principles of Christian growth interact to help us mature in Christ.

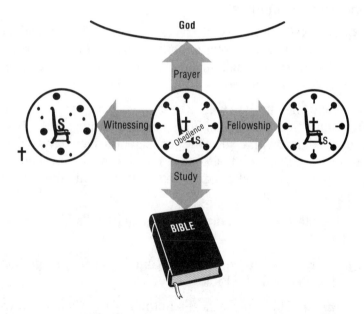

Explain: The first two principles of Christian growth, "We Must Read the Bible" and "We Must Pray," help us deepen our relationship with God. This could be called our vertical relationship. Through the Bible, God communicates to us. Through prayer, we communicate with Him.

The next two principles, "We Must Fellowship with Other Christians" and "We Must Witness for Christ," help us reach out to others. This could be called our horizontal relationship. In fellowship, we communicate with other Christians about our Savior and the bond He gives us with one another. In witnessing, we communicate with non-Christians. We tell them about Jesus, what He has done for us, and what He desires to do for them.

Principle five, "We Must Obey God," is the core of our growth. As we obey Christ, we experience increasing joy, peace, and fellowship with the Lord Jesus Christ and fellow believers. And we become increasingly more mature in our Christian walk.

Application (8 minutes)

Explain: A simple and yet marvelous way in which we can get to know God better is through spending time alone with Him, reading His Word, and talking to Him in prayer. This is often referred to as a "quiet time."

Generally, the morning will be best for you when you're fresh, before your active day begins. For some, the evening is the best time to spend time with God as they consider the next day's plans. Whatever the time, be consistent in meeting with Him. Let me give you some practical suggestions to make your quiet time meaningful.

1. *Pray:* Start with a short prayer asking God's blessing on your time with Him.

2. *Read:* Begin with the Gospel of John if you are just getting acquainted with the Bible.

3. *Meditate:* This simply means to think seriously about spiritual things. Meditate deeply and quietly on what you are reading and how it applies to your life.

   Questions for meditation:

   - Is there a special promise to claim?

   - What insight am I given into myself and my life situation?

- What does Christ require of me now in thought, word, or action?

- Is God pointing out something in my life that is displeasing to Him?

4. *Pray:* Talk to God. Praise and worship Him. Tell Him about the things you have done and said and thought for which you are sorry. Thank Him for all He has done, for all He is doing, and for all He will do for you. Pray for your family, for friends, neighbors, co-workers, and acquaintances, and for yourself. **Write the following points on your flip chart.**

Use the ACTS method to help you talk to God.

A—*Adoration*	To adore God is to worship and praise Him.
C—*Confession*	Tell Him about the things you have done and said and thought for which you are sorry (1 John 1:9).
T—*Thanksgiving*	Thank Him for all He has done, for all He is doing, and for all He will do for you.
S—*Supplication*	Pray for your family, for others, for yourself.

Go through the chart to help your students plan a quiet time for the next week. Encourage them to use this chart regularly.

My Quiet Time with God							
Day	Sun.	Mon.	Tue.	Wed.	Thur.	Fri.	Sat.
Date							
Time							
Prayer requests							
Bible passage							

Explain that writing down prayer requests will help them see how God answers their prayers. Remind them to thank God for these answered prayers. Suggest that they begin reading one chapter in the New Testament each day.

Specific Prayers Made	Date of Prayer	Date of Answer
1.		
2.		
3.		
4.		
5.		
6.		

Closing and Prayer (5 minutes)

Ask your group members what has been most helpful to them from the five-week Bible study. What would they change? Jot down their answers to help you in your next *Five Steps* Bible study. Thank them for their involvement in the group. Answer any questions they may have about the material you have covered.

Close with a prayer like this:

Father, we thank You for these five weeks in which we have learned to grow as Christians. Thank You for the ways we are now prepared to grow further. Continue to teach us through Your Word under the guidance of the Holy Spirit. In Jesus' name. Amen.

Student Lesson Plan

Read 2 Peter 3:18. What is the result of spiritual growth?

Principle One: We Must Read the Bible

1. Jesus said, "Man shall not live by bread alone." How did He say that we should live and be nourished? (Matthew 4:4)

2. The Bible is often referred to as "the Word of God" because it contains God's words to us. Why is reading God's Word so important? (2 Timothy 3:16,17)

3. What will result in your life when you read God's Word? (Psalm 119:11,105)

Principle Two: We Must Pray

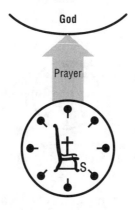

When praying, remember these things:

1. Pray about everything. (Philippians 4:6,7)

   What is the result if we talk to God about everything?

2. Pray specifically. (John 14:14, 16:24)

   Why do you think it is important to pray specifically?

   What will be two results of praying specifically?

3. Pray continually. (1 Thessalonians 5:17)

   What does the Bible mean when it says to pray continually?

Principle Three: We Must Fellowship With Other Christians

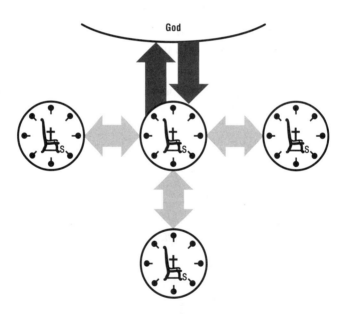

1. As God's children, what should we not neglect? (Hebrews 10:24,25) Why?

2. What are the basic functions of a local church? (Colossians 1:25–28; 2 Timothy 4:2)

3. The new believers in the early church continued steadfastly in what four things? (Acts 2:41,42)

   a.

   b.

   c.

   d.

4. If we spend 90 percent of our time with non-Christians and 10 percent with Christians, which group will have the greater influence on our lives? Why?

Principle Four: We Must Witness for Christ

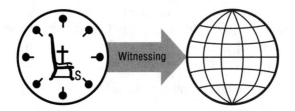

One of the greatest acts of obedience is to share Christ with others in the power of the Holy Spirit. How did the first-century Christians obey the command to witness? Read Colossians 1:28,29 and answer the questions.

1. What did Paul and the other believers do everywhere they went?

2. Why did they do this?

3. Where did they get the power to do this?

Romans 3:21–25 tells us what our message should be to those who do not know God personally. Read the verses from the *Living Bible*, then fill in the blanks.

1. In Romans 3:21, God says we cannot get to heaven by _____ or by trying to keep His _____.

2. Romans 3:23,24 tell us that _____ have sinned and yet now God declares us not _____ if we _____ in Jesus Christ, who in His kindness freely takes away our _____.

3. Romans 3:25 says that God sent _____ to take the _____ for our sins and to end all God's anger against us. He used Christ's _____ and our _____ as the means of saving us from His wrath.

Answer the following questions.

1. What is the greatest thing that has ever happened to you?

2. What, then, is the greatest thing that you can do for another person?

3. In Romans 1:14–16, Paul tells us his own attitude about sharing the good news of Jesus Christ with others. Using his three "I's" as the keys to the passage, describe his attitude in your own words.

4. What was Jesus' promise in Acts 1:8?

Write down the names of several people with whom you plan to share your faith in Christ during the next week.

_____   _____

_____   _____

Principle Five: We Must Obey God

1. How can you prove that you love the Lord? (John 14:21)

2. What will be the result of keeping Christ's commandments? (John 15:10) What does that mean to you?

3. Where do we get the power to obey God? (Philippians 2:13)

4. In light of Christ's illustration in Luke 6:46–49, why would you say that obedience to Christ is imperative for your life?

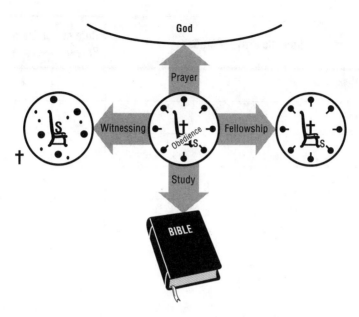

Fill out the first chart to plan your quiet time for the next week. Use the second chart on page 104 during your quiet time.

My Quiet Time with God							
Day	Sun.	Mon.	Tue.	Wed.	Thur.	Fri.	Sat.
Date							
Time							
Prayer requests							
Bible passage							

Specific Prayers Made	Date of Prayer	Date of Answer
1.		
2.		
3.		
4.		
5.		
6.		

Have You Heard
of the
Four Spiritual Laws?

Just as there are physical laws that govern the physical universe, so are there spiritual laws that govern your relationship with God.

LAW ONE

GOD **LOVES** YOU AND HAS A WONDERFUL **PLAN** FOR YOUR LIFE.

God's Love

"God so loved the world that He gave His only begotten Son, that whoever believes in Him should not perish, but have eternal life" (John 3:16).

God's Plan

[Christ speaking] "I came that they might have life, and might have it abundantly" [that it might be full and meaningful] (John 10:10).

Why is it that most people are not experiencing the abundant life?

Because...

LAW TWO

MAN IS **SINFUL** AND **SEPARATED** FROM GOD. THUS HE CANNOT KNOW AND EXPERIENCE GOD'S LOVE AND PLAN FOR HIS LIFE.

Man Is Sinful

"All have sinned and fall short of the glory of God" (Romans 3:23).

Man was created to have fellowship with God; but, because of his own stubborn self-will, he chose to go his own independent way and fellowship with God was broken. This self-will, characterized by an attitude of active rebellion or passive indifference, is an evidence of what the Bible calls sin.

Man Is Separated

"The wages of sin is death" [spiritual separation from God] (Romans 6:23).

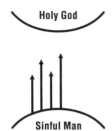

This diagram illustrates that God is holy and man is sinful. A great chasm separates the two. The arrows illustrate that man is continually trying to reach God and the abundant life through his own efforts: good life, ethics, philosophy, and more.

The Third Law gives us the only answer to this dilemma...

LAW THREE

JESUS CHRIST IS GOD'S **ONLY** PROVISION FOR MAN'S SIN. THROUGH HIM YOU CAN KNOW AND EXPERIENCE GOD'S LOVE AND PLAN FOR YOUR LIFE.

He Died In Our Place

"God demonstrates His own love toward us, in that while we were yet sinners, Christ died for us" (Romans 5:8).

He Rose from the Dead

"Christ died for our sins... He was buried... He was raised on the third day, according to the Scriptures... He appeared to Peter, then to the twelve. After that He appeared to more than five hundred..." (1 Corinthians 15:3–6).

He Is the Only Way to God

"Jesus said to him, 'I am the way, and the truth, and the life; no one comes to the Father but through Me'" (John 14:6).

This diagram illustrates that God has bridged the chasm that separates us from Him by sending His Son, Jesus Christ, to die on the cross in our place to pay the penalty for our sins.

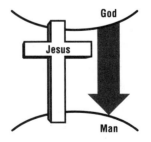

It is not enough to know these three laws...

LAW FOUR

WE MUST INDIVIDUALLY **RECEIVE** JESUS CHRIST AS SAVIOR AND LORD; THEN WE CAN KNOW AND EXPERIENCE GOD'S LOVE AND PLAN FOR OUR LIVES.

We Must Receive Christ

"As many as received Him, to them He gave the right to become children of God, even to those who believe in His name" (John 1:12).

We Receive Christ Through Faith

"By grace you have been saved through faith; and that not of yourselves, it is the gift of God; not as a result of works that no one should boast" (Ephesians 2:8,9).

When We Receive Christ, We Experience a New Birth

(Read John 3:1–8.)

We Receive Christ Through Personal Invitation

[Christ speaking] "Behold, I stand at the door and knock; if any one hears My voice and opens the door, I will come in to him" (Revelation 3:20).

Receiving Christ involves turning to God from self (repentance) and trusting Christ to come into our lives to forgive our sins and to make us what He wants us to be. Just to agree intellectually that Jesus Christ is the Son of God and that He died on the cross for our sins is not enough. Nor is it enough to have an emotional experience. We receive Jesus Christ by faith, as an act of the will.

These two circles represent two kinds of lives:

Self-Directed Life
S – Self is on the throne
† – Christ is outside the life
● – Interests are directed
    by self, often resulting
    in discord and
    frustration

Christ-Directed Life
† – Christ is in the life
    and on the throne
S – Self is yielding to Christ
● – Interests are directed
    by Christ, resulting
    in harmony with
    God's plan

Which circle best represents your life?

Which circle would you like to have represent your life?

The following explains how you can receive Christ:

YOU CAN RECEIVE CHRIST RIGHT NOW BY FAITH THROUGH PRAYER

(Prayer is talking with God)

God knows your heart and is not so concerned with your words as He is with the attitude of your heart. The following is a suggested prayer:

> *Lord Jesus, I need You. Thank You for dying on the cross for my sins. I open the door of my life and receive You as my Savior and Lord. Thank You for forgiving my sins and giving me eternal life. Take control of the throne of my life. Make me the kind of person You want me to be.*

Does this prayer express the desire of your heart?

If it does, pray this prayer right now, and Christ will come into your life, as He promised.

How to Know That Christ Is in Your Life

Did you receive Christ into your life? According to His promise in Revelation 3:20, where is Christ right now in relation to you?

Christ said that He would come into your life. Would He mislead you? On what authority do you know that God has answered your prayer? (The trustworthiness of God Himself and His Word.)

The Bible Promises Eternal Life to All Who Receive Christ

"The witness is this, that God has given us eternal life, and this life is in His Son. He who has the Son has the life; he who does not have the Son of God does not have the life. These things I have written to you who believe in the name of the Son of God, in order that you may know that you have eternal life" (1 John 5:11–13).

Thank God often that Christ is in your life and that He will never leave you (Hebrews 13:5). You can know on the basis of His promise that the living Christ indwells you and that you have eternal life from the very moment you invite Him in. He will not deceive you.

Note: All Scripture references are from the *New American Standard Bible*.

Resources to Help You
Lead Your Bible Study

Transferable Concepts. Exciting tools to help you experience and share the abundant Christian life. These booklets explain the "how-to's" of consistent, successful Christian living. Use for personal study, follow-up, and discipling others.

How You Can Be Sure You Are a Christian
Resource for Lesson 1

How You Can Experience God's Love and Forgiveness
Resource for Lesson 2

How You Can Be Filled With the Spirit
Resource for Lesson 3

How You Can Walk in the Spirit
Resource for Lesson 4

How You Can Be a Fruitful Witness
Resource for Lesson 5

How You Can Introduce Others to Christ
Resource for Lesson 5

How You Can Help Fulfill the Great Commission

How You Can Love By Faith

How You Can Pray With Confidence
Resource for Lesson 5

How You Can Experience the Adventure of Giving

How You Can Study the Bible Effectively

Ten Basic Steps. A comprehensive curriculum for the Christian who wants to master the basics of Christian growth. Used by hundreds of thousands worldwide. Study Guides and Leader's Guide available.

Study Guides: Eleven individual booklets

Introduction: The Uniqueness of Jesus

Step 1: The Christian Adventure
Resource for Lesson 1

Step 2: The Christian and the Abundant Life

Step 3: The Christian and the Holy Spirit
   Resource for Lesson 3

Step 4: The Christian and Prayer

Step 5: The Christian and the Bible

Step 6: The Christian and Obedience

Step 7: The Christian and Witnessing
   Resource for Lesson 5

Step 8: The Christian and Giving

Step 9: Exploring the Old Testament

Step 10: Exploring the New Testament

Leader's Guide: The ultimate resource for those who want to lead a Bible study. Contains study outlines, questions and answers from the Study Guide, and leader's instructions for teaching the complete series. An easy-to-use guide for even the most inexperienced, timid person asked to lead a group study.

A Handbook for Christian Maturity: Combines the entire series of the *Ten Basic Steps* in one volume. A handy resource for private or group Bible study. An excellent book to help nurture spiritual growth and maturity, this time-tested handbook has helped millions around the world discover the secret of abundant life.

A Man Without Equal (video). Intriguing 30-minute video explores the uniqueness of Jesus through dramatic recreations and breathtaking portraits from the great Masters. An effective evangelism tool, giving viewers an opportunity to receive Christ. Excellent for Sunday school, group meetings, or personal study. This video can be used to help start your Five Steps group.

A Man Without Equal (book). A fresh look at the unique birth, teachings, death, and resurrection of Jesus and how He continues to change the way we live and think. Excellent as an evangelistic tool. Readers are given an opportunity to receive Christ.

Life Without Equal. Discover purpose, peace, and power for living. A presentation of the length and breadth of the Christian's freedom in Jesus Christ and how believers can release Christ's resurrection power for life and ministry. Good for unbelievers or Christians who want to grow in their Christian life. *Resource for Lesson 5*

Four Spiritual Laws booklet (pkg. of 50). One of the most effective evangelistic tools ever developed. An easy-to-use way of sharing your faith with others. An estimated 1.5 billion copies have been distributed in all major languages.

Would You Like to Know God Personally? booklet (pkg. of 50). An adaptation of the *Four Spiritual Laws.* Presents four principles for establishing a personal relationship with God through Jesus Christ.

Spirit-Filled Life booklet (pkg. of 25). Discover the reality of the Spirit-filled life and how to live in moment-by-moment dependence on Him.

The Secret. An inspiring book showing you how to discover a new dimension of happiness and joy in your Christian walk and draw upon the purpose, power, and guidance of the Holy Spirit.

Witnessing Without Fear. A step-by-step guide to sharing your faith with confidence. Ideal for both individual and group study. A Gold Medallion winner.

Keys to Dynamic Living (3×5 card; pkg. of 15). An excellent reminder of how to experience a joyful, fruitful, Spirit-filled life. Gives key points to act upon in dealing with temptation and restoring the fullness of God's Holy Spirit in your life. Small enough to tuck into your pocket, purse, or Bible. Use for follow-up on new believers, in your Sunday school class, or give to family members and friends.

Available through your local Christian bookstore, mail-order catalog distributor, or NewLife Publications.

BILL BRIGHT is founder and president of Campus Crusade for Christ International. Serving in 152 major countries representing 98 percent of the world's population, he and his dedicated associates of nearly 50,000 full-time staff and trained volunteers have introduced tens of millions of people to Jesus Christ, discipling millions to live Spirit-filled, fruitful lives of purpose and power for the glory of God.

Dr. Bright did graduate study at Princeton and Fuller Theological seminaries from 1946 to 1951. The recipient of many national and international awards, including five honorary doctorates, he is the author of numerous books and publications committed to helping fulfill the Great Commission.